The Vis

SW

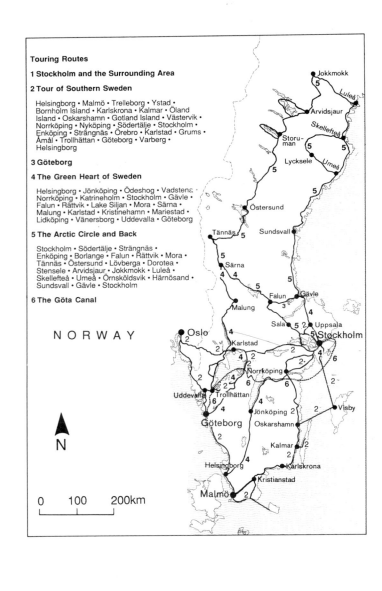

Touring Routes

1 Stockholm and the Surrounding Area

2 Tour of Southern Sweden

Helsingborg • Malmö • Trelleborg • Ystad •
Bornholm Island • Karlskrona • Kalmar • Öland
Island • Oskarshamn • Gotland Island • Västervik •
Norrköping • Nyköping • Södertälje • Stockholm •
Enköping • Strängnäs • Örebro • Karlstad • Grums •
Åmål • Trollhättan • Göteborg • Varberg •
Helsingborg

3 Göteborg

4 The Green Heart of Sweden

Helsingborg • Jönköping • Ödeshog • Vadstena •
Norrköping • Katrineholm • Stockholm • Gävle •
Falun • Rättvik • Lake Siljan • Mora • Särna •
Malung • Karlstad • Kristinehamn • Mariestad •
Lidköping • Vänersborg • Uddevalla • Göteborg

5 The Arctic Circle and Back

Stockholm • Södertälje • Strängnäs •
Enköping • Borlange • Falun • Rättvik • Mora •
Tännäs • Östersund • Lövberga • Dorotea •
Stensele • Arvidsjaur • Jokkmokk • Luleå •
Skellefteå • Umeå • Örnsköldsvik • Härnösand •
Sundsvall • Gävle • Stockholm

6 The Göta Canal

N O R W A Y

N

0   100   200km

THE
VISITOR'S GUIDE TO
SWEDEN

MPC

HUNTER
PUBLISHING INC

British Library
Cataloguing in Publication Data

Lange, Hannes
    Visitor's guide to Sweden.
    1. Sweden—Description and travel—
    1945—Guide-books
    I. Title II. Schweden. *English*
    914.85'0458   DL607

Author: Hannes Lange
Translator: A.J. Shackleton

© Goldstadtverlag   Karl A. Shäfer,
    Pforzheim
© Moorland Publishing Co Ltd
    1987 (English edition)
Reprinted 1991

Published by
Moorland Publishing Co Ltd,
Moor Farm Road,
Airfield Estate,
Ashbourne, Derbyshire
DE6 1HD, England

ISBN 0 86190 173 8 (paperback)

Published in the USA by
Hunter Publishing Inc,
300 Raritan Centre Parkway,
CN94, Edison, NJ 08818

ISBN 0 935161 14 7

Printed in the UK by
Butler and Tanner Ltd, Frome, Somerset.

Cover photograph: *Gripsholm
Castle, Mariefred* (Peter Baker,
International Photobank).

The rest of the black and white
and colour photographs were
supplied by the Swedish
National Tourist Office.

CONTENTS

Key to Symbols Used in Margin

⌘   Items of historical or cultural interest.

     A beautiful view or interesting natural phenomenon.

The Routes

On the pages which follow, the names of the most important places on the routes have been entered in the margin, together with the distances between them. Recommended excursions and detours are also included.

INTRODUCTION TO SWEDEN

1. The Country and its People

Geographical Situation

The kingdom of Sweden is the largest of the Scandinavian countries. It has an area of 450,000sq km, which is about twice that of the United Kingdom; but with 8.32 million inhabitants it has only 15 per cent of the population of the UK and only about 4 per cent of the population of the USA. Sweden has a population density of nineteen inhabitants per sq km, compared with 251 per sq km in the UK, 13 per sq km in Norway and 14 per sq km in Finland. 8.6 per cent of the total land area (38,700sq km) is made up of lakes, of which there are about 100,000 altogether; half of the total land surface is covered with forests.

Over 80 per cent of the population live in towns, and almost half of these live in or around Stockholm, Göteborg (Gothenburg) or Malmö, or in the Östergötland region between Lake Vättern and the towns of Linköping and Norrköping. 86 per cent of the population live south of the 61st parallel (running through Lake Siljan), although the area of the country to the north of here is almost twice that of the country to the south.

The northernmost point of Sweden is where the three countries of Sweden, Norway and Finland meet. These are the only two countries to share borders with Sweden (1,800km with Norway and 400km with Finland). The sea coast is longer than the land borders, being roughly 2,500km long. It is bounded on the west by the Skagerrak and the Kattegat, and on the east by the Baltic Sea and the Gulf of Bothnia. If all the many inlets and islands are taken into account, the coastline is actually as long as 7,500km.

The land frontiers with Norway and Finland are less of a barrier to traffic than other borders within Europe, because the Scandinavian countries are in customs union with each other. Minor border crossings have no more than one customs officer either side of the frontier, and are often not even manned at all.

Half of Sweden is covered by forest

Once a visitor has crossed over into Scandinavia, there are very few formalities at any of the borders, and none at all for the Scandinavians themselves.

Sweden is a long country: the most southerly town is Trelleborg at 55°20', while the northernmost point is at 69°4', well north of the Arctic Circle and as far north of Trelleborg as Naples is to the south! Sweden is almost 1,600km long from north to south. The length of the country brings about problems of transport and communication. There are also vast climatic differences between north and south. Summer in the north is fairly warm and sunny, but lasts barely 2 months; and the land is covered with ice and snow for as many as 8 months of the year. On the other hand, the fertile southern province of Skåne has a climate which differs little from that of Central Europe.

However, even the northern part of Sweden is covered in thick forests, which are of great economic importance, while many areas in Russia to the east are covered in tundra, with barely enough vegetation to support reindeer. This is due to the warming effect of the Gulf Stream, for although Sweden has no Atlantic coast, it is only divided from the Atlantic Ocean by the thin strip of northern Norway.

Southern Sweden is a green and fertile area similar to Denmark, with prosperous farmsteads, pretty farm cottages and an almost park-like landscape. Further north in central Sweden, and especially towards the Norwegian border, the land is wilder and more mountainous. But even here the forests and moorlands are interspersed with fertile agricultural regions such as Dalarna — the so-called green heart of Sweden.

The 61st parallel running through Lake Siljan is the point at which northern Sweden begins — the country of eternal forests, wild rivers and innumerable lakes. The far north of Scandinavia is the home of the Lapps, of whom about 10,000 live in Sweden. They are Europe's only nomadic race, and are called the *Sameh* in their own language.

The far north is also where Sweden's greatest mineral resources are to be found, in the iron-mining region around Kiruna. It is interesting to note that the iron ores are not exported via Swedish ports on the Gulf of Bothnia, but are carried by rail along the famous iron-ore line to Narvik on the Norwegian coast. This is because the Gulf of Bothnia becomes iced up, while the Norwegian coast remains ice-free throughout the winter.

In spite of the length of their country, the Swedes are a remarkably united race, if one discounts the 10,000 Lapps and the 50,000 Finns that inhabit the far north. Sweden resembles Norway and Finland in terms of its landscape and settlement patterns, and also in the character of its people; and yet when one crosses into Sweden its well-kept towns and villages have perhaps, a more distinctive air of affluence. This impression remains throughout the whole of Sweden.

The far north of Sweden towards the Norwegian border is characterised by Alpine-type scenery, and includes Sweden's highest mountain, Kebnekaise (2,123m). The popular areas for winter sports are in north-western and central Sweden, where the skiing season often extends well into the summer months.

The transport problems posed by Sweden's geographical situation have been resolved by modern technology. Sweden's rail network includes 12,000km of line, and all the main routes are electrified. All major regions are served. The road network is also well-constructed, and although one Swede in four owns a car, it is possible to travel on good country roads for hours at a time without meeting a single other vehicle. Air traffic has increased enormously in recent years, and carries three times as many

Small planes are necessary transport in Northern Sweden

passengers and five times as much freight as in the mid-1970s.

The Swedish merchant fleet amounts to 1 per cent of the world total, and includes an unusually large number of recently-built ships. A large proportion of the internal trade, especially that of wood, makes use of the inland waterway system. The most important waterway is the Göta Canal, which was built in the last century. It is 596km long, running from Göteborg on the Kattegat to Stockholm, the capital, which is also the most important Baltic port. Only 196km consists of actual canals, the rest being made up of rivers and various lakes (see page 161).

Geographical Regions

Sweden is divided into three main geographical regions, which in turn are divided into twenty-four provinces. The northern region is **Norrland**, which approximately occupies the area north of the 61st parallel. It covers more than half the total area of Sweden, but includes less than 15 per cent of the population. The Norrland region is divided into nine provinces: Lapland, Jämtland and Härjedalen to the west; Norrbotten (North Bothnia), Västerbotten (West Bothnia), Ångermanland, Medelpad, Hälsingland and Gästrikland to the east. It is a region of vast impenetrable forests, high mountains and fast-flowing rivers.

Sweden's west coast

The northernmost province of Lapland is situated at the edge of forests, where birchwoods gradually give way to the high tundra — the habitat of the Lapps and their reindeer herds. The area around Kiruna is of great economic importance with its rich deposits of iron ore. The lakes and rivers of the far north are frozen over for much of the year. The trees are felled during this period and the trunks are brought down and laid on the ice. They are then carried downstream with the meltwater in the spring. These rivers are being increasingly harnessed for power stations, which fulfil the majority of the country's energy needs.

The central region of Sweden is called **Svealand**, which includes the seven provinces of Dalarna (Dalecarlia), Värmland, Västmanland, Närke, Uppland and Södermanland. Svealand forms the cultural and historical core of Sweden. The climate is milder and pleasanter than further north. There are as many as 20,000 islands along the east coast, which look particularly impressive from the ferry that comes in from Finland to Stockholm. The ship approaches the harbour along an inlet filled with a vast number of islands. Not for nothing has this region been

Norrviken Gardens, Båstad, Skåne

called the 'land between earth and water'. For the Baltic Sea is linked to the Kattegat via the complicated system of lakes, rivers and canals which bounds the region to the south.

Further north, the forests become denser as the scenery becomes wilder, culminating in the beautiful province of Dalarna in the region of Lake Siljan. Here the traditional forestry and wood-processing industries are now being supplemented by tourism.

The southern part of Sweden is known as **Götaland** after the ancient Goths who are supposed to have settled here (though this is not proven). Götaland is made up of the eight provinces of Västergötland, Östergötland, Småland, Skåne (Scania), Blekinge, Dalsland, Bohuslän and Halland, plus the islands of Gotland and Öland. This region resembles central Germany, and is mostly covered by forests interspersed with peatlands. The areas around the great lakes of Vänern, Vättern and Mälaren are well-served by waterways such as the Göta Canal. They form an important industrial region, which is world-famous for its precision industries. Norrköping is a textile-manufacturing centre, while Götaland is also the location for most of Sweden's famous glassworks. Göteborg (Gothenburg) is the most important port to the west, and also manufactures machines and cars (including Volvo). Skåne, on the other hand, has an almost Danish feel to it,

Folk-dancing in national dress

being a lush and fertile region covered with farms and large modern agricultural concerns. It also has many parks and estates. The warmer and sunnier west and south coasts, together with the islands of Gotland and Öland, have a large number of popular seaside resorts.

Also typical of the region are the plush little wooden cottages with rust-red paint that are scattered all over the countryside.

The Swedish People

Although Sweden covers such a large area, its people are remarkably alike in character. The Swedish are somewhat middle-class in their attitudes, and have made great social and technological advances in recent decades. This is true as much in the country as in the towns. Swedes are often pictured dressed in colourfully embroidered jackets with clogs and plus-fours, but such costumes are only to be seen at traditional festivals in certain provinces such as Dalarna.

Most Swedes tend to be serious and matter-of-fact, and although quiet and reserved, they are friendly by nature. The isolation of the countryside makes them a very hospitable race, and in few other places is one so well-received. Their isolation also tends to make for individualism, which is as true of the Swedes as it is of other Scandinavians. They often behave with a certain rough-and-ready informality, which is sometimes mistakenly thought of as showing a lack of courtesy. Conversely, the Swedes themselves often find others somewhat affected in their manners. Both are purely a matter of social convention.

The Swedes have a great respect for one another's property. Thefts and burglaries are mostly confined to the towns, while in the country people tend to leave their cars and houses unlocked. No one worries if a postman leaves a parcel beside a postbox, even if it is miles from the lonely farmstead to which it belongs.

The standard of living is, and incomes generally are, relatively high, but the correspondingly high cost of living means that a higher proportion of women go out to work than in most other Western European countries. One result of this is that women's liberation is not considered a problem in Sweden. Women's rights are recognised as a matter of course, and duties are more equally divided between the sexes. Another result is that with both parents at work the young tend to be left more to themselves. This makes for greater independence but also for greater rebelliousness. The result is a worrying increase in juvenile crime and drug addiction.

Not all Swedes are tall and fair-haired. Swedes have always welcomed immigrants, so that their Nordic blood has been mixed with that of other races. Until recently the number of immigrants has always been exceeded by those emigrating to North America and Australia. But nowadays the tide has turned thanks to Sweden's advanced social order, and immigrants far outnumber those leaving the country. In the northern provinces there are about 10,000 Lapps and 50,000 indigenous Finns, all of whom are Swedish citizens. Of the 380,000 naturalised immigrants, about half have come over from Finland. There are about 414,000 other immigrants, most of whom are guest workers.

Although Sweden covers such a large area, its local dialects are less sharply differentiated than those of Norway. But there is a bigger difference than in English between the spoken language (talspråk) and the written language (riksspråk). The dialects in the south are closer to Danish, while those in the north and east have a number of features in common with Norwegian. The Finns and Lapps in the north have their own mother tongues, but learn Swedish as their first language at school. English is compulsory in all Swedish schools, with German as the second language. So visitors should have no problems in making themselves understood. The first word they will learn on arriving in Sweden is 'Hej! ' — the normal Swedish greeting.

Old Lapp

The Lapps in Sweden

Visitors to northern Sweden, and especially to the province of Lapland, will invariably come in contact with members of what is probably the most remarkable race in Europe. Known as the *Sameh* in their own language, the Lapps are fully aware of how strange their culture and way of life appears to most Europeans, and use this knowledge to their advantage. The Swedish government also grants them special status, which is laid down in law.

The Lapps are easily distinguishable from their fellow countrymen, both in their brightly-coloured costumes and in their physical appearance. The costume which is usually associated with the Lapps is in fact their normal winter clothing, which in the summer is only worn for the benefit of tourists. It usually consists of a blue jacket with bright red trimmings, beautifully embroidered breeches, reindeer-skin boots and a pointed cap, the design of which varies according to the clan. As regards their physical appearance, the Lapps are dark-haired with mongoloid features and yellow-brown skin; they are short and stocky and are rarely more than 160cm (5ft 3in) tall.

They have lived in northern Scandinavia since time immemorial, and are believed to have migrated from east of the Urals at least two thousand years ago. They have lived in northern Sweden for so long that they have a fully recognised claim to make use of the land. They occupy the whole of northern Scandinavia. They originally lived from fishing and hunting, for reindeer in particular. After that they began to herd the reindeer, and since then their way of life has remained unchanged for nearly

Reindeer, Saltoluokta, Lapland

a thousand years. Their population is now estimated to be about 40,000, of whom about 10,000 live in Sweden. Because of their independent and nomadic way of life, it is difficult to produce exact figures. However, of those 10,000 living in Sweden, there can be no more than 2,000 (about 600 families) who are still herding reindeer.

Most Lapps nowadays have turned to other forms of livelihood, and some have left their traditional homelands. The degree of assimilation varies, from those who adhere closely to their Lapp traditions, to others who have adapted completely to the Swedish way of life. In recent years, however, the Lapps have become more conscious of their heritage, thanks partly to the interest shown in them by tourists, and partly to encouragement from the government.

Some of the reindeer herdsmen have given up their nomadic existence, and have developed ways of farming reindeer in permanent pastures, usually in the more wooded regions, and often in combination with other forms of livestock. The rest, however, still keep to their tents as they follow the wandering herds across the far northern wastes of Scandinavia. In the winter they come south again, irrespective of national frontiers. In the mountain foothills, where the reindeer breed, the Lapps have gradually set up more permanent camps, where they spend the spring and autumn in a more settled environment. The families often stay there permanently, while only the active herdsmen wander off with the reindeer.

Dog sleds have now been replaced by motorised ones, or by cars or even helicopters. In the old days each family owned a small herd, which they used for milk, meat and skins, and also as beasts of burden; whereas nowadays all the reindeer are bred together in large herds, and are kept primarily for their meat. Each animal bears the mark of its owner, usually stamped on its ear and before the animals are moved into their winter camps, they are sorted into individual herds. This 'division of the reindeer' has now developed into a large folk festival, which attracts spectators from a wide area.

The skins and the antlers, which are borne by both sexes, are also used for commercial gain. The Lapps show great craftsmanship and artistic talent in the articles which they produce for sale. The skins are made into shoes and into nicely-designed rugs, while the antlers are turned into beautifully carved souvenirs for the tourists.

The Swedish government has set up a commission to investigate the social and cultural problems of the Lapps, especially now that fewer of them remain with the reindeer herds.

There has also been a great interest shown in the language of the Lapps. They have virtually no written literature, but like the Eskimos they have a strong oral tradition which finds its expression in the *Joiken* — ancient ballad-like songs.

Children of resident Lapps attend schools in the settlements where they live, while those of nomadic families are usually sent to one of the eight state schools that have been set up specially for them. The choice lies with their parents. The schools are the same as others in Sweden, except that they also teach the language and culture of the Lapps.

The Lapp college at Jokkmokk has been going for over forty years. This is where adult Lapps can catch up on the education they have missed, or else continue their education. The agricultural authorities have also organised special courses in reindeer husbandry.

Such measures have been instituted, both in Sweden and in the adjoining Lapp regions of Norway and Finland, so as to preserve the culture and identity of the Lapps.

The Constitution

Sweden is a constitutional monarchy and parliamentary democracy. The Social Democrats have been the strongest political party for the majority of the last forty years, and though they are committed to the creation of a republic, there are no signs that this change will ever come about. The constitutional power is divided between the government and parliament; since the constitutional reform of 1975, the king has retained only a symbolic and representative role as head of state. The parliament is made up of five political parties: the Social Democrats, the Centre Party, the Liberals, the Conservatives and the Communists. Apart from the Communists, there are no major differences between the parties except on the issue of nuclear energy, which brought about an election defeat for the Social Democrats in 1976. They are now in power again however, with Ingvar Bengtsson as prime minister.

The royal family have belonged to the Bernadotte dynasty since 1810, when they were elected to follow the Vasas, who had died without issue. Gustav VI Adolph was king of Sweden from 1950 until his death in 1973 at the age of 91. His son had died in an aeroplane accident in 1947, so he was succeeded by his 27-year-old grandson Carl XVI Gustav. In 1976 King Carl Gustav married a German, Silvia Sommerlath. The throne has always been passed down the male line in the past, but the present heir is the king's daughter Victoria. The royal family lives in the relatively unpretentious style typical of Scandinavian royalty.

The constitutional reform of 1971 brought about a change from a two-chamber to a single-chamber parliamentary system, and the number of elected representatives was reduced to 349. Of these, 310 are elected directly by their constituencies, while the remaining 39 are appointed according to the proportion of votes for each party overall. The Swedish government, or state council as it is called in Sweden, is chaired by the prime minister, who is authorised by the king to form a government. He is always the leader of the largest party in parliament. Local government is exercised by the provincial councils and the parish or town councils. Parliamentary and local elections take place on the same day. The trade unions have enormous power in Sweden,

Crown Regalia,
Royal Palace,
Stockholm

both in the indirect political influence which they wield and in the vast economic assets which they hold.

Sweden is one of the richest countries in the world; its per capita gross national product is seventh in the world. Income levels are relatively high and differentials are low. However, the cost of living is correspondingly high. It is not cheap to live in Sweden, and national insurance contributions are high.

About 20 per cent of public spending is on the social and welfare services. All Swedish citizens receive a statutory old age pension from the age of 67. This is further supplemented, depending on an individual's previous income and national insurance payments. Sweden has a full national health service. All medical bills above a certain threshold are paid for by the state. Dental treatment, however, is not included in this. National insurance contributions are levied together with income tax.

The Educational System

Swedish children attend school from the age of 6 for a minimum of 9 years. The subjects studied are the same for all children for the first 6 years. English is compulsory from the fourth year onwards. In their seventh year, children may choose either technical or

Lund University

language options, and German is usually offered as the second foreign language. Pupils who wish to continue their education have three options to choose from. The first of these is 3 years at what is effectively the equivalent of a British sixth-form college, which entitles them to a university education. Alternatively, they may go to a technical college and obtain qualifications of a more vocational kind; this may also lead on to further courses of study. The third option is a specialist vocational school, in which the practical learning for specific jobs is combined with the appropriate theoretical training.

Apart from a very few exceptions, all Swedish schools and universities offer free education with all books and equipment provided. A free school meal is also available. The school day is from 8am to 4pm with an hour's break for lunch. Children who continue at school from 16 to 18 receive a yearly allowance from the state of about 1,000 skr. University students receive maintenance grants; these are partly in the form of a loan, which they must later repay.

Sweden has six universities: Stockholm, Göteborg, Malmö, Uppsala, Lund and Umeå. There are about 120,000 students in all. On matriculation they are issued with special white caps, which they wear throughout their period as undergraduates; these are an everyday feature of Swedish life.

Natural Resources

Sweden's natural resources are of three kinds: forests, minerals and water power. At one time the forests were Sweden's only known natural asset. The trees that are felled are mostly coniferous, and are carefully protected from over-exploitation. The number of trees felled is enormous, but it is matched by a corresponding reafforestation programme. There are vast areas of forest, especially in the north, that have never seen an axe. On the other hand, the short growing season means that the trees grow more slowly than in Central or Western Europe. They must therefore be allowed to grow for between 90 and 150 years before they are ready to be felled. But the slow growth rate also produces a high-quality wood. Forty-five million cubic metres of timber are felled every year, which is still about 15 per cent below the annual replacement rate. Sweden is the world's sixth-largest timber producer.

The timber is transported along the many rivers and

waterways. During the winter the logs are carefully marked to show whom they belong to, and carried out onto the ice which covers the rivers and lakes. In the spring they are either carried downstream with the meltwater, or else tied together into enormous rafts and transported along lakes and canals to specific destinations. Nowadays Sweden exports very little unprocessed wood. The wood is mostly processed by various companies and co-operatives in factories all over the country.

The rich iron-ore deposits of Swedish Lapland have only been exploited during the last 50 years, since there had previously been no way of refining this particular kind of ore. The best ores are to be found near Kiruna, where they have an iron content of nearly 70 per cent. But there are also some important deposits in the Grengesberg area of central Sweden. The most valuable ores are exported, mostly via the Norwegian port of Narvik. In recent years, however, the Swedes have begun to refine the ores themselves. A total lack of coal resources meant that previously there had not been enough energy available, but the vast increase in hydroelectric power has now made it possible. However, the recent steel crisis has been followed by a slump in world demand for iron.

Sweden has a large number of fast-flowing rivers, which form a vast source of energy. Hydroelectricity has now become Sweden's number-one energy resource, and its production is still being increased. This development will unfortunately involve sacrificing a number of famous landmarks such as the waterfalls at Trollhättan.

Industry

In the last hundred years, Sweden has changed from an agrarian to an industrial economy. The oldest industry is that based on wood. Apart from chipboard, plywood and furniture, cellulose and paper are also produced. Some of the goods are exported, while others are made into finished products by the Swedes themselves. Swedish paper is always of high quality, right down to the paper towels in hotels and chalets.

One more recently introduced industry involves the production of steel by electrochemical means. Swedish steel has gained a reputation for high quality, and its stainless steel products have become part of everyday life. The steel industry is based mostly in southern and central Sweden, especially in the neighbourhood of the Göta Canal and the three great lakes. The steel produced here has become world-famous, as have the products made out of it, such as car and ship engines (Volvo, Saab and Scania), ball-bearings and other precision products.

The products of the electrical industry are similarly world-renowned (Electrolux). The chemical and plastics industries are also important, and are closely associated with Alfred Nobel, the inventor of dynamite.

Agriculture

A land which covers such a large area naturally supports a variety of agricultural activities. The rich farmlands of Skåne in the south, with their modern cultivation methods, form a stark contrast to the small mountain crofts in the north, which have nothing but Alpine pastures. Agricultural firms have overcome the country's transport problems by forming into large co-operatives, which are now responsible for 90 per cent of Sweden's agricultural output. Apart from the fertile grainlands of the south, Sweden's

Farmland in Östergötland

agriculture is almost exclusively devoted to livestock. This forms 80 per cent of total output, and is almost equally divided between dairy and meat production.

Sweden produces nearly all of its food requirements; over and above that, it produces a number of high-quality items, such as special kinds of bread and frozen foods, which it exports all over the world. Of the various grain crops, wheat is the most important, but other crops such as oats, rye and barley are also grown. Further exports are produced from these, such as porridge oats and a wide variety of crispbreads.

Art and Culture

A language with only 8 million speakers is not likely to have a very large literary output, but Sweden has produced a few important literary figures. Nothing of significance was written before about 1700, and the first writer of note was Carl Michael Bellman

Selma Lagerlöf, authoress

Carving 'Dala Horses', Dalarna

(1740–95), whose highly sentimental poetry is typical of the Rococo period. German romanticism and French classicism both came over to Sweden in the early nineteenth century, and there was much rivalry between proponents of the two schools. Nothing of significance is left from this period. It was quickly followed by the awakening of Swedish nationalism, which harked back to the ancient Norse culture. The most famous work of this period was the *Fridtjof Saga* by Esaias Tegener (1782–1846).

C. J. L. Almkvist (1793–1866) was the first to write novels incorporating social critique.

The turn of the century was the golden age of Swedish literature. Rydberg, Levertin, Fröding and Snoilsky have all produced works which have been translated into English. But by far the greatest of them was the dramatist August Strindberg (1849–1912). The poems of Selma Lagerlöf (1858–1940) were inspired by the beautiful scenery of Dalarna. Her most famous works were probably *Little Nils Holgersson's Wonderful Journeys* and *Gösta Berling's Saga*. The writers who followed concentrated on the *genre* of the realistic novel; they included A. A. Karlfeld, Gustaf Gejerstam, Ellen Key and Hjalmar Söderberg. Well-known contemporary writers include Nobel prizewinner Pär Lagerkvist, lyric poet Bo Bergmann and young people's author Astrid Lindgren.

Sweden has a rich tradition of visual art. The Swedes, like the Norwegians, have a particular liking for sculpture. The ancient runestones from the Viking period show how skilled the Scandinavians have always been at carving stone. Thanks to the abundance of wood, there was a long tradition of wood carving, most of which has sadly been lost due to fire. The first stone carvings go back to the tenth century; they can be seen in the famous Romanesque cathedral at Lund and in the abbey at Vadstena. The cathedrals at Uppsala and Skara, and the Storkyrkan in Stockholm, are examples of the Gothic style which was introduced from northern Germany. Very little early sculpture remains, but it includes the famous wooden statue of St Birgitta in Vadstena Abbey.

Swedish painting has a long tradition going back to the prehistoric rock drawings of Bohuslän. Architecture flourished especially in the seventeenth century, when the Swedish nobility gained enormous fortunes in the Thirty Years' War. This resulted in magnificent palaces such as the great Riddarhuset in Stockholm. The end of the nineteenth century saw another great flowering of the visual arts, with painters such as Carl Hill and Andreas Zorn, and sculptors such as Carl Milles, whose reputation has gone far beyond the boundaries of Scandinavia.

Swedish music has never been very important outside Sweden itself. Folk music has always flourished, but relatively little classical music has been produced. One of the best-known composers was Hugo Alfven, who wrote *Swedish Rhapsody*. On the other hand, Sweden is much better known in the field of musical performance. There are several symphony orchestras, the best-known being the Stockholm Philharmonic. The opera houses of Stockholm, Göteborg and Malmö all give outstanding performances. Since 1973 Abba has put Sweden on the map in the the pop world. Sweden's theatrical achievements have also been considerable. Recent years have seen a number of famous producers and directors, such as Ingmar Bergman, Arne Sucksdorff, Alf Sjöberg and Arne Mattson.

The press is very important in Sweden. It enjoys complete freedom, and has a surprisingly large readership in proportion to the population. This is true of both national and local papers. One in every two Swedes buys a newspaper every day, and it is normal to buy a local as well as a national paper. Radio and television are also very important. Thanks to the high standard of living, almost every household has at least one of each. The whole country is served by transmitters. Programmes include a high proportion of documentaries, and there are no advertisements.

Religion

Ninety-two per cent of the population belong to the Protestant Lutheran Church, whose head is the Archbishop of Uppsala. It is financed by a system of church taxes, which are collected by the state. The church at one time played a very important role in the life of the community, especially in country areas. But now, as in other countries, attendances are continually falling. The Protestant Free Churches are active in Sweden, with about 400,000 members in all. The Roman Catholic Church numbers no more than about 80,000 members, most of whom are from immigrant families.

Some Facts About Sweden

Constitution:	monarchy with parliamentary government	
Area:	449,964sq km	
Population:	8.3 million	
Population density:	18.5 inhabitants per sq km	
Length:	1,600km as the crow flies	
Coastline:	2,500km; including irregularities 7,500km	
Borders:	with Sweden 1,800km with Finland 400km	
Latitude:	southernmost point 55°20' northernmost point 69°4'	
Most important lakes:	Vänern	5,546sq km
	Vättern	1,900sq km
	Mälaren	1,140sq km
	Hjälmaren	484sq km
	Storsjön (Jämtland)	456sq km
	Siljan (Dalarna)	354sq km
	Torneträsk (Lapland)	322sq km
Most important rivers:	Klarälven-Götaälven	720km
	Muonio-Torneälven	570km
	Dalälven	520km
Highest mountains:	Kebnekaise (Lapland)	2,123m
	Sarjektjåkko (Lapland)	2,090m

	Helagsfjället (Hjärjedalen) 1,796m
	Storsylen (Jämtland) 1,762m
Land use:	arable and pasture land 9.9 per cent; forests 50 per cent; barren land and lakes 40.1 per cent
Landscape:	flat agricultural land in the south, mountains and forests in central Sweden, high mountains in the north-west, east coast rocky and very irregular
Main imports:	crude oil and oil products, iron and steel, cars and lorries, animal skins, fruit, coffee, luxury goods
Main exports:	wood, cellulose, paper, iron ore, machines and instruments, chemical products
Industries:	metals and machine building 46 per cent; forestry and wood processing 15.1 per cent; textiles and clothing 9.3 per cent; food production 8.2 per cent; chemicals 5.4 per cent; glass and ceramics 4.6 per cent; other industries 6.6 per cent
Religion:	Protestant Lutheran 92 per cent; Free-church Protestant 5 per cent; Roman Catholic 1 per cent
National flag:	yellow cross on a blue background

2. A Short History

The Swedes were first mentioned in about AD100 by the Roman author Tacitus. This was about the time when Germanic tribes were moving north into Scandinavia, displacing the indigenous peoples, who were probably the ancestors of the Finns. The people who settled in Skåne were closely related to the Danes; the Götar settled further north in Gotland, while the Svear settled in the area around Lake Mälaren, where Stockholm is situated today. These three main tribes fought against each other for supremacy, which according to the saga was eventually won by the Svear at the Battle of Bråvalla in 750. They gave their name to the whole country.

During the Viking period, between 830 and 1200, Sweden was gradually being Christianised. The Vikings came mostly from Norway and Denmark, and conquered parts of southern and central Sweden. Joined by some of the more adventurous Svear, the Vikings travelled to Eastern Europe, Britain and France, and even to Sicily and North America. King Olav Eriksson was baptised as a Christian in about 1008. In 1157 King Erik IX began the conquest of Finland. One of Sweden's first statesmen was Birger Jarl, who acted as a kind of regent, endeavouring to secure the stability of the realm. He died in 1266.

Engelbrekt the Liberator, Arboga

In 1397 in the Union of Kalmar, Sweden came under the rule of Queen Margaret of Denmark. This personal union was looked on by the Swedes as a form of foreign oppression. In 1433 a miner called Engelbrekt Engelbrektsson led an uprising against the Danes. This was the first of many attempts by Sweden over the next 100 years to gain independence from the union. In 1435 the Swedes formed their own parliament, and in 1448 they chose Carl VIII Knudson as their king in opposition to Denmark. In 1471 the Swedish army under Sten Sture beat King Christian I of Denmark at the Battle of Brunkeberg. 1477 saw the founding of the first Swedish university at Uppsala.

In 1520 Sten Sture was beaten by King Christian II of Denmark, and the leaders of the Swedish rebellion were executed in the so-called Stockholm Bloodbath. In 1521, however, Gustav Vasa gathered a peasant army at Lake Siljan in Dalarna, and drove the Danes out of most of Sweden. He was made king in 1523, and reigned until 1540.

In 1527, Sweden joined the Reformation. In the decades which followed, she began to build an empire across the Baltic. Sweden's power continued to grow under Gustav II Adolf (1611–32), who supported the German Protestants in the Thirty Years' War. He fell in 1632 at the Battle of Lützen. He was succeeded by his daughter Christina. Chancellor Oxenstierna took over the leadership, and continued the Swedish expansion. He drove the Danes out of Jämtland and Gotland, and also took over Bremen and Verden in Germany, together with areas of Pomerania.

Carl X Gustav (1654–60) finally drove the Danes out of Skåne and Halland. His successor Carl XI came to the throne at only 4 years of age, and in 1675 the Swedes were beaten at Fehrbellin by the Grand Elector of Brandenburg. Between 1700 and 1718, his successor Carl XII fought in Russia, Poland, Denmark and Norway, and eventually fell in Norway in 1718. Between 1719 and 1721, Sweden was forced to give up most of her Baltic possessions, leaving only Finland and Pomerania.

In 1807 King Gustav IV Adolf joined the Napoleonic Wars; he lost Pomerania, and 1809 he lost Finland. He was deposed, and his uncle became King Carl XIII. He died without issue and in 1810 the Swedish parliament elected Marshal Jean-Baptiste Bernadotte of France to succeed him. Bernadotte took the title of King Carl XIV Johan, and in 1813 led the Swedish troops against Napoleon. This was the last war that Sweden took part in. In 1814

Sweden gave up Pomerania but gained Norway.

In the decades which followed, the Bernadotte monarchs strengthened the country by means of circumspect politics. Under Oskar I (1844–59), Carl XV (1859–72) and Oskar II (1872–1907), Sweden pursued a policy of strict neutrality. In 1905, under pressure from growing opposition, Oskar II dissolved the union with Norway. His successor Gustav V reigned until 1950 and kept Sweden out of both World Wars. Gustav VI Adolf (1950-73) continued the policy of neutrality. Sweden joined the United Nations in 1946 and the Council of Europe in 1949, but stayed out of NATO in order to preserve her neutrality. Since 1959, Sweden has been a member of EFTA, the European Free Trade Association. King Carl XVI Gustav succeeded his grandfather in 1973, but since the constitutional reform of 1975 he retains no more than symbolic power.

3. The Geology of Sweden

If one looks at a map of Sweden, one can see that its geology can only be understood in relation to the whole of the Scandinavian peninsula. The land slopes gradually towards the east from a mountain chain running along the western frontier, which reaches its highest point in the north west; the southern part of the country is relatively flat.

The region is, geologically speaking, very old. The mountain range in the west, which lies mostly in Norway, is a remnant of the great Caledonian fold mountain range, which was formed in the Silurian Period. It is mostly made up of Pre-cambrian rocks such as granite and gneiss — some of the oldest rocks in the world.

For about a million years, Sweden was covered by an ice sheet up to 2,000m thick. It melted about 8,000 years ago, thousands of years after the ice age was over in Britain. This glaciation had a dramatic effect on the landscape. The soil was taken away, and was replaced by rocks and stones brought down by the glaciers from the mountains. Thus the whole of Sweden was strewn with rocks which were rounded and eroded by the ice.

The melting of the glaciers caused the sea level to rise so that the Baltic Sea became connected with the Gulf of Bothnia and the North Sea. At the same time, however, the land, which had been weighed down by the ice sheet, began to rise as well, and is still

'Raukar' or rock pillar, Gotland

rising to this day. The coast of northern Sweden is rising by as much as a centimetre a year in places, while the Stockholm region has risen 40cm in the last century. The result is that many of the port installations have continually had to be moved — at Luleå, for example.

The glaciers also gouged out deep hollows; these were later flooded to form the many lakes which give the Swedish landscape

Drottningholm, Stockholm

Sweden, land of forests and waterways

A Småland village

its particular character. The whole country is covered with moraines — piles of debris left behind by the glaciers. This is the reason why much of the land not covered by lakes is unsuitable for crops or pasture.

As the ice gradually melted, it formed rivers which flowed east into the Gulf of Bothnia. These rivers still serve to carry the spring meltwaters eastwards from the western mountains down to the gulf. They run through dense coniferous forests, and form the natural transport routes for the trees which are felled.

Apart from the high mountains towards the north and west, Sweden is not a very mountainous country. The climate and the geology of the country have greatly influenced the landscape, from the farmlands of the south, via the dense coniferous forests of central and northern Sweden, to the stunted birchwoods of Lapland. South of the Dalälv, which runs into Lake Siljan, the conifers are mixed with deciduous woodland, giving the beautiful province of Dalarna its distinctive character.

4. Climate and Travel

It almost goes without saying that the best time to travel in Sweden, as elsewhere in Scandinavia, is during the summer

View from Mount Isaberg, Småland

	Average temperatures				Average precipitation		Sunshine in hours per year
	January		July				
	°C	°F	°C	°F	cm	in	
Malmö	0	32	17	63	56	22	1,900
Stockholm	−3	26	18	64	56	22	1,700
Kiruna	−12	10	13	55	51	20	2,000
Edinburgh	3	37	15	59	70	27	1,300
Manchester	5	41	16	61	86	34	1,200
London	5	41	18	64	59	23	1,500
Paris	3	37	19	66	59	23	1,800
Hamburg	0	32	17	63	74	29	1,400
Munich	−2	28	17	63	94	37	1,700
New York	1	34	25	77	112	41	2,500
Madrid	4	39	24	75	43	17	2,900

months of June, July and August. Summer in Sweden tends to be sunny and dry. The days are long, with hardly any darkness to speak of, while northern regions enjoy the midnight sun.

A country that extends so far north is inevitably subject to great climatic differences. While northern Lapland has an average January temperature of 5°F, that of Stockholm is only 26°F. Winter begins very early in the north: the birch trees of Lapland begin to turn brown even in August, while the night frosts set in at the beginning of September. The Skåne region is influenced by the Gulf Stream, and rarely has winter averages below freezing. Spring usually begins here in mid-March. Central Sweden does not see the end of winter until the second half of April, while spring in Lapland is as late as the end of May or early June. But the further north one goes, the sharper the transition from winter to summer.

Nature makes up for these short summers by means of a vigorous growing season. A snow covering can be replaced in only a few days by a carpet of flowers. And although the far north experiences the lowest winter temperatures, the continental nature of the climate can produce summer maxima of 86°F or more that are hardly ever experienced in southern Sweden.

However, the summer climate of Sweden is quite pleasant on the whole, and the heat is never unbearable. The inland lakes warm up very late and are often still covered by ice when the first bathers venture into the sea off the south coast. But the long, sunny days quickly warm the surface of the lakes and provided there is no strong through-current, the surface waters become pleasantly warm while the deeper water remains cold.

Another good time to travel is the early autumn, at the beginning of September. It is too cold for bathing, but the weather remains sunny and is well suited to touring Sweden by car.

5. The Midnight Sun and the Northern Lights

The phenomenon of the midnight sun can be fairly easily explained. The earth turns on its axis once every 24 hours, and at any moment half of the earth is receiving light from the sun. One might think that this should produce exactly 12 hours of daylight and 12 hours of darkness, but in fact this is only the case on the equator — the point mid-way between the two poles. This is because the earth is tilted on its axis: from April to September the northern hemisphere is tilted towards the sun, while from October to March it is tilted away. The combination of this factor with the rotation of the earth means that, while at the equator day and night are equal, their length varies increasingly as one travels towards the poles. This is what produces the seasonal changes, both in daylight and climate.

The result of all this is that in a certain area around the North Pole, the sun in midsummer is still above the horizon at midnight; conversely, in midwinter the sun never rises at all. At the South Pole the seasons are of course the opposite way round. Now the earth's axis is tilted at an angle of 23° 27'; so, bearing in mind that the equator is at 0° and the North Pole at 90°, there must be a line at 66°33' where the sun shines all night at midsummer (the night following 23 June). This line is known as the Arctic Circle. The period of the midnight sun increases towards the North Pole. Thus at Kiruna it shines from 31 May to 16 July, while at the North Cape in Norway it shines from 13 May to 30 July. But even southern Sweden, like Scotland, has as much as 20 hours' daylight at midsummer, while at Stockholm the midsummer night lasts for no more than about 2$\frac{1}{2}$ hours.

People are affected by this phenomenon as much as animals and plants. At midsummer, the whole of Scandinavia is full of life and vitality. People need less sleep and are much more excitable. It is the time of festivities, especially in Sweden. Meanwhile in the north the plant world has exploded into life. The time between bud, blossom and fruit, which in Britain can take anything up to 6 months, is, in northern Sweden, concentrated into the space of 3 or 4 weeks.

Another strange northern phenomenon is that of the northern lights. People have speculated for centuries as to the cause of this terrifying spectacle. The sky is first lit up with yellow and red light, and is then filled with a dazzling medley of bands of light, varying enormously in colour, shape and intensity. The whole night sky is lit up like a great theatre, with hundreds of enormous spotlights, shining as if through a veil of diaphanous curtains. Sometimes the sky almost looks to be on fire. It is not surprising that the northern lights were once greatly feared as an omen of great evil.

The cause of the northern lights is still not yet fully understood. (They should properly be called polar lights, since they occur towards the South Pole as well.) They appear to be associated with sunspots — explosive disturbances on the surface of the sun. These sunspots send massive waves of protons and electrons (subatomic particles) out into space, which hurtle towards the earth at almost the speed of light. As they enter the earth's magnetic field, the particles are deflected towards the poles. This is why these lights occur most frequently near the magnetic poles, though they may occasionally be seen further south (or north). When the particles reach the outer edge of the atmosphere (between 100km and 1,000km above the earth), they cause ionisation and give off large amounts of light. The colours produced vary enormously, and the result is the glorious spectacle known as the northern lights. (Neon lights are an example of ionisation on a much smaller scale.)

1 STOCKHOLM AND THE SURROUNDING AREA

Stockholm is Sweden's capital and seat of government, and with a population of 900,000 it is also Sweden's largest city. The built-up area includes twenty-five towns with an overall population of 1.5 million. The city is spread out over 24,000 rocks and islands between Lake Mälaren and the Baltic Sea, and covers a total area of 6,500sq km. The administrative area straddles the two provinces of Södermanland to the south and Uppland to the north, with the provincial boundary going right through the city centre.

Stockholm in Brief

Stockholm is commonly known as the Venice of the North, because like Venice it is full of waterways and islands. One important difference, however, is that the water is clean enough for bathing and fishing. Nearly a third of the city is made up of parks and green areas. Its beautiful setting makes it one of the most delightful cities in Europe, and yet it still possesses all the bustle and variety of a major world city.

The **old city** (Gamle Staden) is known by the Swedes as *staden mellan broarna* or 'the city among the bridges'. The 700-year-old heart of Stockholm is fascinating with its narrow streets and historic buildings. It is also full of restaurants and shops selling souvenirs and specialist goods.

Just north of here is the modern city centre of **Norrmalm**. With its many tall modern buildings, it is full of life and vitality. It shows Sweden at its most modern, and possesses all the flair of a bustling new metropolis.

The island of **Djurgården** is devoted entirely to leisure pursuits, including a pleasure park, several famous museums and many beautifully kept parks. It also possesses one of Sweden's greatest attractions — the zoo and the Skansen open-air museum.

There is also much to see in the surrounding area: the Stockholm archipelago, Lake Mälaren, the towns of Vaxholm,

Sigtuna and Södertälje, and the many local castles and palaces.
A whole week is needed to do justice to the city and its environs.
However, 2 or 3 days will be enough to visit just the main sites in
the city.

The History of Stockholm

The Stockholm area has been inhabited since prehistoric times,
though Birka and Sigtuna were originally the main settlements on
Lake Mälaren. But when the harbour at the then capital of Sigtuna
became silted up, the small trading post at Stockholm gained in
importance. It was fortified in 1252 during the regency of Birger
Jarl. The increasing trade enabled Stockholm to grow, and the fort
was turned into a castle. In 1336, Magnus Eriksson was the first
king to be crowned in the cathedral.

Stockholm, built on fourteen islands

In the mid-fourteenth century, Stockholm suffered much competition from the Hanseatic League. Danish expansionism led to the outbreak of war, and between 1389 and 1395 the city was regularly under attack from these southern neighbours. Sweden was absorbed into Denmark in the Union of Kalmar in 1397, and the city of Stockholm dwindled in importance. The Swedes began a long and bloody struggle against the Danish monarchy, which came to a head with the invasion of King Christian II in 1520. The Danish monarch ignored all pleas, and had eighty nationalists executed in the famous Stockholm Bloodbath. But this did not break the Swedish resolve, and in 1523 Gustav Vasa and his army of peasants liberated the city from its unpopular foreign rulers.

Under the Vasa monarchs, Sweden grew into an empire, with Stockholm more and more at its centre. Johan III built some magnificent buildings, shipbuilding developed under Gustav II, and the government was gradually moved to Stockholm. But it was not made the official Swedish capital until 1634. The population grew fast, from 9,000 in 1630 to 40,000 only 40 years later.

Stockholm did not, however, escape the usual disasters of the Middle Ages. Several great fires destroyed most of the wooden houses, and in 1697 the Castle of the Three Crowns (*Tre Kronor*) also fell victim to fire. In 1710 the city was decimated by the plague. But the city remained untouched by war, and after the liberation of 1523 it was never again invaded by a foreign army.

In the sixteenth century, Stockholm became the academic centre of Sweden. 1730 saw the founding of the Royal Academy of Science and the Royal Observatory. Several more colleges followed. The 'modern era' began in the mid-nineteenth century with the advent of gas lighting, which was followed 10 years later by the coming of the railways. 1891 saw the opening of the world's first open-air museum at Skansen. The 1912 Olympic Games were held at Stockholm In 1956, Stockholm hosted the Olympic equestrian events, which had been banned from Melbourne because of Australia's stringent quarantine regulations. The first underground line was opened to traffic in 1950, while the trams have been running since 1877.

In the last 30 years, the city's skyline has been transformed by a large number of modern buildings. But these vast glass and concrete edifices have not robbed the city centre of its charm. For modern Stockholm is a marvellous example of the fact that the architecture of the 70s and 80s need not be impersonal.

Things to See in Stockholm

Most visitors to Stockholm will be interested to see different things. So instead of a suggested tour, the sights are divided up according to the parts of the city where they are located.

Tourist Information

Before embarking on a tour of the city, visitors are recommended to enquire at the Swedish Tourist Board at Hamngatan 27 (on the corner with Kungsträdgårdsgatan — see page 45). This provides ample information about what there is to see, plus a good map of the city (which is essential). There is also a recorded telephone service in English.

The Old City

The Royal Palace (Kungliga slottet)
This massive seventeenth-century Renaissance building contains 608 rooms altogether. Three floors are open to the public

Changing of the guard

provided there are no official engagements. The following rooms are of particular interest: the Bernadotte Rooms, including the guardroom; the Columned Hall and the Victoria Hall; the reception rooms of King Oskar II and Queen Sophie; the Blue and Red Drawing Rooms; and the magnificent dining hall. The guest rooms are on the second floor. The north wing contains the eighteenth-century state apartments, of which the Carl XI Gallery is probably the most impressive room in the palace.

The Ministerial Hall is where every government is sworn in by the monarch. The following are also worth seeing: the Imperial Courtroom with its silver throne; the Treasury, containing the ceremonial swords of Gustav Vasa among other insignia; the Royal Armoury, with its hunting weapons, state carriages and ceremonial armour; the Palace Museum, which depicts the various stages in the building of the palace; Gustav III's Museum of Antiquities, with sculptures and antique vases collected by the monarch himself; and finally the Palace Chapel with its eighteenth-century interior.

Stockholm Cathedral (Storkyrkan)

The cathedral with its 56m high tower is the oldest building in the city. It was founded by Birger Jarl in 1260 at the same time as the city itself, and was dedicated to St Nicolas of Myra, the patron

*Stortorget, Old City,
Stockholm*

saint of seafarers. It was added to in the fifteenth and sixteenth centuries, and was refurbished in the Baroque style in the eighteenth century. All kings after Gustav Vasa were crowned here until Gustaf V abolished the ceremony. But special services still take place here in the presence of the royal family.

To the north of the altar is a famous late Gothic wooden sculpture of St George and the Dragon. It was carved in 1489 by Bernt Notke from Lübeck in Germany, and is one of the masterpieces of medieval wood carving. It was given to the church by Sten Sture after his victory over the Danes in 1741. Also worth seeing is the reredos from 1652, which is made out of silver, ebony and ivory. The 300-year-old royal throne was made by Nicodemus Tessin the Younger. The picture above the organ staircase is the oldest known representation of Stockholm. Ehrenstrahl's *Last Judgement* is one of the largest paintings in the world. The crucifixion painting on the east wall is by the same artist. The nave contains the tombs of famous families, including that of the Reformer Olavus Petri and the Tessin Grave designed by Carl Milles in 1933.

The Great Market (Stortorget)

This historic square surrounded by lovely medieval buildings is the place where the Stockholm Bloodbath took place on 8 November 1520. One of the buildings standing next to it is the **Exchange** (Börshuset), built in 1773, which is probably the finest Rococo building in Stockholm. The stock exchange still takes place every weekday morning on the ground floor. The rooms on the upper floors are occupied by the Swedish Academy and the Nobel Library. This is also where the Academy meets to allocate the Nobel Prizes. Other old buildings on the square include the Grillskahus and the Schantzkahus.

The German Church (Tyska kyrkan)

This late Gothic church was founded in the sixteenth century by the German Hansa merchants, who dedicated it to St Gertrude. It was extended to its present form in about 1640. The steeple is 92m high. The interior is Baroque, and is beautifully decorated with works by German masters.

The Knights' House (Riddarhuset)

This seventeenth-century mansion is one of the finest examples of the late Dutch Renaissance style. Chancellor Oxenstierna commissioned Simon de la Vallée to build it in 1641. On his death, its building was taken over by architects Heinrich Wilhelm and Joost Vingboons, and it was finished in 1674 by Jean de la Vallée, the son of the original architect. Until 1866 it was used as an assembly hall by the nobility. The magnificent rooms are open to the public. The Knights' Hall contains the 2,325 coats of arms of all the Swedish noble families. The impressive ceilings were painted by Ehrenstrahl. In front of the Knights' House is a statue of Gustav Vasa, which was made by L'Archevesques in 1774.

Riddarholmen

Wrangel Palace

This palace was built for Count Karl Gustav Wrangel in the mid-seventeenth century. It was designed by Tessin the Elder and Jean de la Vallée. The count was born in 1613 at the family home of Skokloster Castle (see page 86), and was supreme commander during the Thirty Years' War in Germany. When the Royal Castle was burnt down in 1697, the royal family was given temporary shelter here in what was then the finest building in the city. The building was later altered, and now houses the Stockholm Supreme Court.

Riddarholm Church

This church was first completed in the early fourteenth century, and originally belonged to a Franciscan friary. It has been considerably altered and extended down the centuries. Since the seventeenth century it has been the burial place of the Swedish monarchs and of deserving citizens of the realm. It includes the Carolingian Vault, the Gustavian Burial Chapel and the Chapel of the Bernadottes, and also the tombs of Magnus Ladula and Karl Knutsson. Seventeen monarchs are buried here altogether. The walls are hung with the coats of arms of the Seraphin Knights, who were knights of the Franciscan order.

Birger Jarl's torg

This square has one or two historic buildings such as the Stenbock Palace, and also the remains of the fifteenth-century fortifications, including Birger Jarl's Tower.

Helgeandsholmen

The Parliament Building (Riksdagshuset)

Riddarholm Church, Stockholm

This massive structure completely dominates the small island of Helgeands-holmen between Norrmalm and the old city. It was built at the beginning of the century. The Swedish Parliament has had to move out several times during recent years while the building was being renovated. It adjoins the old Imperial Bank, which now also houses government offices.

Norrmalm

The Modern Centre
Stockholm's main modern shopping centre lies between Sergel's torg and the Hötorg. Hötorgshallen, the underground market, is linked via subways and pedestrian ways to the Sergelsarkaden and the **main station**. The Hötorg (Haymarket) is the site of the modern **concert hall**, where the Nobel Prizes are distributed. In front of it is the famous Orpheus Fountain, which was created by Milles in 1936. Sergel's torg is dominated by the impressive **Kulturhus** (House of Culture) and the large modern fountain. Not far away is the **tourist information office** (see page 40).

Adolf Fredrik's Church
This church is just north of the Hötorg in Holländargatan. It was built in 1774 in the Baroque style. It contains sculptures by J. T. Sergel, who is buried in the churchyard. One of these is an epitaph to the philosopher Descartes. The beautifully decorated

Parliament Building

The National Museum

dome is also very impressive.

The Strindberg Museum
Situated in Drottninggatan is the so-called Blue Tower, which was
the last residence of the dramatist August Strindberg (1849-
1912). The house has been made to look just as it did between
1908 and 1912, when the poet was still living there. It contains
original furniture and ornaments, some of which were donated by
Strindberg's descendants. The museum also includes a library, a
newspaper and picture archive and a lecture theatre, which is
also used for music and drama evenings. A few of Strindberg's
paintings are also on show, which bear witness to his abilities as
an impressionist painter.

Hologram Gallery
The Hologram Gallery is near the Strindberg Museum in Drottninggatan, and is only the fourth of its kind to have been opened in the
world. Amongst the three-dimensional pictures, the portrait
collection is particularly remarkable.

St Clare's Church (Klarakyrkan)
This church is just east of the main station in Klarabergsgatan.
The original church was built at the end of the sixteenth century

on the site of a thirteenth-century nunnery of the Order of St Clare. It was burned to the ground in 1751, and was rebuilt 2 years later in the Gustavian style. The 104m high tower was erected in 1880. The old vestry has been turned into a museum, which includes a collection of liturgical objects and garments. In the churchyard is the grave of the singer Carl Michael Bellman (1740–95).

Gustav Adolf's torg

In the square opposite the island of Helgeandsholmen is an equestrian statue of King Gustav Adolf, which was sculpted by L'Archevesques. To the east is the **Royal Opera House**, which was built in 1898 in the Renaissance style, while the building to the west is the **Crown Prince's Palace**, which nowadays houses the foreign ministry. North of the square is **St James's Church**, a small church in the late Gothic style.

The Mediterranean Museum (Medelhavsmuseet)

Originally housed in the Historical Museum, the Mediterranean Museum now has its own building on Gustav Adolf's torg. It includes the famous Cyprus Collection with its terracotta figurines. There is also an Egyptian section containing mummies and sarcophagi, and a section on Islamic culture.

The Hallwyl Museum

This is housed in Hamngatan in a palace built by Count Hallwyl at the turn of the century. The building is almost in its original state, and is filled with a large and varied collection of lovely treasures, which originally belonged to the countess herself.

Kungsträdsgården

These gardens contain a statue of Carl XIII and a monument to Carl XII. There is also an open-air theatre, together with a number of restaurants and snack bars.

The National Museum

This massive building in Södra Blasieholmshamnen was built in 1866. It houses the largest art collection in Sweden, with works spanning the last 500 years. The original collection went back to the previous century, with significant contributions from Gustav III. It eventually grew too large to be housed in one place, so it was divided up, and the applied art, sculpture and painting collections were kept at the National Museum site.

The first floor includes applied art, furniture, tapestries, glass, porcelain and silver from Sweden and elsewhere in Europe. The second floor is devoted entirely to paintings. It includes many works by important Swedish artists such as Roslin (*The Veiled Lady*), Sergel, Richter, Larssen and Zorn. The European section includes paintings by Rembrandt, Rubens, Chardin and Renoir, to name but a few.

Skeppsholmen

Skeppsholm Church
Skeppsholm Church was built in the style associated with Carl Johan, and is also known as Carl Johan's Church. Building was started at the beginning of the nineteenth century, but the church was not finished until 1842.

The Far Eastern Museum (Östasiatiska museet)
This museum, to the north of the island, has been considerably altered and extended in recent years. It contains a large collection of eastern art and handicrafts from various centuries, including Chinese porcelain, Japanese watercolours and Indian Buddhas. It also boasts the largest collection of Stone Age pottery outside China. One recent addition is Gustav VI Adolf's famous Chinese collection.

Museum of Modern Art (Moderna museet)
Opposite the Far Eastern Museum is the Museum of Modern Art, which shows all the very latest in contemporary art. There is always something new and interesting in the temporary exhibitions and at the special events which are organised.

The museum also houses permanent collections of contemporary Scandinavian art. Surrealism, Dadaism, abstract art and pop art are all represented. The most prized items are works by Picasso, Dali and Matisse, and by the late Andy Warhol, that guru of pop art.

Also attached are the Museum of Photography, a film club and a children's film club.

Museum of Swedish Architecture
(Svensk Arkitektur museet)
This museum presents a comprehensive account of Sweden's architectural achievements over the last 100 years by means of sketches, photographic prints, transparencies and models. Temporary exhibitions provide insights into the planning problems facing the architects of today.

The Skeppsbron and youth hostel Chapman

The sailing boat moored outside the museum is called the **Chapman**. It now serves as a rather unusual youth hostel.

Östermalm

The Royal Library (Kungliga bibliotek)
The Royal Library was built in the 1870s, and is situated among the well-kept avenues and lawns of a large park called **Humiegården**. It contains more than half a million volumes, plus countless documents and manuscripts. Among them are the famous *Devil's Bible (Gigas Librorum)* and the *Codex Aureus* — a Latin translation of the Gospels.

The Music Museum
Built in 1640, the former army bakery in Sybillegatan now houses the Music Museum, with a large and varied collection of musical instruments.

The Army Museum
The Army Museum in Riddargatan houses a collection of uniforms, medals, weapons and flags, showing the development

of the Swedish Army from Gustav Vasa down to the present day.

The Royal Drama Theatre
The Drama Theatre is on Nybroplan not far from the Army Museum. This magnificent marble palace was opened in 1907. It is well-known for its interesting and varied programmes.

The Museum of Dance
Situated in Laboratiegatan, the Museum of Dance is full of costumes, masks and decorations. There are video screens on which visitors may watch different kinds of dance being performed.

The Historical Museum
Further out of town on Narvavägen is one of Stockholm's most interesting museums. It is divided into various sections, which together provide a vivid account of life down the centuries. The emphasis is naturally on Swedish history. Exhibits include runestones, tools, ornaments, weapons and a reconstruction of a Viking house.

On the second floor is the Royal Coin Collection, which includes coins, notes and medals of all ages from all over the world.

Norra Djurgården

The Diplomatic Quarter (Diplomatenstaden)
Most of Sweden's foreign embassies are out beyond Östermalm in a beautiful parkland setting. Some of these buildings are quite magnificent. They are heavily though unobtrusively guarded.

Museum of Maritime History (Sjöhistorika museet)
Situated in Djurgårdsbrunnsvägen, this museum documents the history of seafaring and the development of shipbuilding. It includes a unique collection of models of ships from the seventeenth and eighteenth centuries. Even the interiors are modelled closely on the original designs.

The Museum of Technology (Tekniska museet)
Not far away is the Museum of Technology, which displays a magnificent collection of miniature and life-size working models. Of special interest is the mining section, which is appropriately located beneath the museum.

The adjoining building contains the **TV Museum** and the **Electronics Museum**; next door is the **Ethnographic**

Museum, with its collections from all over the world.

Kaknäs Tower

The 155m high television tower to the east of Norra Djurgården is very well worth a visit. Built in 1967, it is the tallest building in Scandinavia, and is of an unusual design. The view from the lookout platform is quite remarkable. The entrance hall contains a Walter Bengtsson relief made out of copper, nickel and enamel. The restaurant seats 200, and is at a height of 120m.

Djurgården

The Nordic Museum

Founded by Arthur Hazelius in 1873, the Nordic Museum is housed in palatial premises to the north of the island of Djurgården. It presents a comprehensive account of the life of the early Scandinavian peoples, with exhibits showing agricultural, fishing, hunting and livestock methods and the folk art of Sweden in particular.

The Biological Museum

The Biological Museum shows the flora and fauna of Sweden in a setting which closely represents the natural environment.

The *Wasa* Museum (Wasavarvet)

The *Wasa* was built between 1625 and 1628 under Gustav II Adolf for use in the Thirty Years' War. This mighty warship was a true giant of its time: 62m long, and weighing 1,300 tonnes, it was armed with sixty-four cannons. On its maiden voyage, however, it capsized before it had even left Stockholm Harbour. Most of the cannons were salvaged, but the ship remained forgotten for more than 300 years, until it was rediscovered by an amateur underwater explorer called Anders Franzén. The hull of the ship was brought up from the seabed in a unique operation, together with 24,000 other items. It was placed in a dry dock, where it has undergone massive restoration; the dock has now become a museum.

Apart from the ship itself, with its massive stern-gallery, there is a large collection of its crewmen's personal effects. A film is shown of how the ship was raised and restored. A visit to the *Wasa* Museum is a must for everyone, and not merely for maritime enthusiasts. It has also become a home for other ships, such as the icebreaker *St Eric* and the *Finngrundet* lightship. They are all in beautiful condition and are open to the public.

Wasa *being transported in 1961*

The Liljevalch Art Gallery
Immediately behind the *Wasa* Museum is an art gallery which is
continually in use for exhibitions of contemporary art.

Gröna Lunds Tivoli
Just south of the *Wasa* Museum is Stockholm's pleasure park.
Gröna Lunds Tivoli includes stalls, broths, restaurants, a circus
and a permanent fair, providing amusement for the people of
Stockholm, both in the evenings and at weekends.

Skansen
Skansen offers such an enormous variety of attractions that
plenty of time is needed to do it justice. The open-air museum was
founded by Arthur Hazelius in 1891, and was the first of its kind in
the world. There are more than 150 buildings altogether. During
the summer months there are demonstrations of traditional
handicrafts as they were once done. The **zoo** is not only the
home of large numbers of native Scandinavian animals; the
aquarium, terrarium and nocturnal animal house include a large
variety of exotic species as well. Lill Skansen is specifically
intended for young visitors, with a children's zoo, a children's play-
ground, roundabouts and a Punch and Judy show among other

Skansen open-air museum

amusements.

There is always something on in the summer at the **Solliden open-air theatre**, including plays, concerts and magic shows. These are only some of the large variety of activities on offer. The site is of course well served with restaurants, snack bars and kiosks.

Rosendal Castle
The eastern part of Djurgården is wilder and more romantic, and it is easy to forget that one is no more than 3km from the city centre. Rosendal Castle was built in 1823 as a summer residence for Carl XIV Johan. It is now a museum, where the empire furniture and period decorations are on show to the public.

Waldemarsudde
In a park at Waldemarsudde, the southernmost point of the island, is an *art nouveau* style villa which originally belonged to Prince Eugen. The prince was not only a talented artist himself, but also gave great support to other contemporary artists. The villa houses a large number of the artist's own works, and the gallery contains one of the finest ever collections of turn-of-the-century

Waldemarsudde villa

Scandinavian paintings.

The Thiel Gallery
The Thiel Gallery is at Blockhusudden at the eastern end of the
island. Built at the beginning of this century by Ferdinand Boberg,
it was commissioned by Ernest Thiel the banker to house his large
private art collection, which includes works by Munch, Nordström,
Fjæstad and Vuillard.

Södermalm

The City Museum (Stadsmuseet)
The City Museum is housed in an old palace just south of the
sluice which separates Lake Mälaren from the Baltic. It is full of
drawings, models, documents and other items illustrating the
history and development of the city.

The Toy Museum
Next to Mariatorget is one of the largest toy collections in the
world. It has over 10,000 exhibits, which are of interest to adults
as well as children. There is also a large model railway which runs
at weekends.

Kungsholmen

Stockholm City Hall
At first sight one is merely struck by the size of this vast brick structure. But it also possesses considerable architectural merit, and is aptly thought of as a symbol of Stockholm. It took 12 years to build, and was finished in 1923. It is made up of about 8 million bricks and more than 19 million little gold mosaic stones. The Golden Hall is particularly impressive, and is used for official receptions. The 106m high tower commands a marvellous view of the city centre.

Brunnsviken

The Natural History Museum
The Natural History Museum is in the northern suburb of Frescati next to Stockholm University. It contains more than 14 million plant and animal exhibits.

The Botanic Garden (Bergianska Trädgården)
Opposite the Natural History Museum and directly by the waterfront is the Botanic Garden. Its hothouses are full of tropical plants, and the Victoria House contains a special attraction — a water lily which is probably the largest in the world.

Other Things to See

Carl Eldh's Studio
The sculptor Carl Eldh had a residence in Lögebodsvägen, which has now been turned into a museum. It still has that 'lived-in' feel about it, and the studio houses all his life's work.

The Postal Museum
Situated in Nygatan, the Postal Museum contains a number of old post vans, plus a magnificent stamp collection including a number of rare stamps.

The Underground (Tunnelbana)
Stockholm's underground system is worth seeing for its own sake. Many of the stations are beautifully designed and decorated, the most impressive being those on the line from Kungsträdgården in the centre to Akalla and Hjulsta. At Odenplan Station there is even a **Tramway Museum**.

Millesgården, Lidingö Island

Things to See Outside Stockholm

Millesgården
Carl Milles' one-time residence is in a beautiful setting on the
island of Lidingö, and has been dedicated to the sculptor's
memory. The terraces are lined with copies of his most famous
works, the originals of which are to be found all over Sweden. The
house and grounds contain other sculptures of his, plus his own
personal collection of works by other sculptors.

Drottningholm Palace
The royal family's residence on the island of Lovön was previously
a summer residence only. The present Baroque structure was
built in the late seventeenth century by Nicodemus Tessin and his
son. The large park has been preserved in its original English and
French form, and is worth a visit for its own sake. The Palace
Theatre, built in 1766, retains its eighteenth-century decor and
possesses the oldest stage machinery in the world. The Chinese
Pavilion in the park contains a valuable porcelain collection and a
Chinese puppet theatre.

The Stockholm Archipelago
There are as many as 24,000 islands and skerries in the area

Vaxholm fortress

between the city and the open sea. They are a paradise for both nature lovers and watersports enthusiasts, which can only be properly appreciated from a boat. A large variety of excursions and ferry services are laid on from Stockholm during the summer months. Islands worth visiting include Själbottna, Gällnö, Ängsö National Park and Bullero, which has a hunting lodge and an exhibition of paintings by Bruno Liljefors.

Vaxholm
The little town of Vaxholm is a busy and popular island resort. The fortress in front of the town has been turned into a museum. Though the island is accessible by road, the best way to get there is on the regular boat service that goes from Stockholm during the summer.

Tyresö Castle
On an island to the south west of Stockholm is a castle that was built for Chancellor Oxenstierna in 1620. The present owner, Claes Lagergren, has turned it into a private museum.

Utö
This island to the south of Stockholm was the site of Sweden's

first iron mine. The only reminders of its industrial past are a few miners' cottages, a mill and a mining museum. The island today is a popular resort, with regular boat services from Stockholm.

Other Places to Visit

There are several other places worth visiting near Stockholm that are described elsewhere in this book. These include the historical and industrial town of **Södertälje** (see page 3), the ancient Swedish capital of **Sigtuna** (see page 112), and **Gripsholm Castle** (see page 111).

2 TOUR OF SOUTHERN SWEDEN

The South Coast and the Major Historical and Cultural Centres

Helsingborg • Malmö • Trelleborg • Ystad • Bornholm Island • Kristianstad • Karlskrona • Kalmar • Öland Island • Oskarshamn • Gotland Island • Västervik • Norrköping • Nyköping • Södertälje • Stockholm • Enköping • Strängnäs • Örebro • Karlstad • Grums • Åmål • Trollhättan • Göteborg • Varberg • Helsingborg

What the Route Has to Offer

This suggested tour covers the whole gamut of what southern Sweden has to offer, both on the coast and inland. Visitors who come via Denmark will be able to compare the two countries. The route also goes close to the Norwegian border, with a suggested detour via Oslo. The tour can thus be combined with holidays in both Norway and Denmark. Although Helsingborg has been chosen as the starting point, the route is circular, so visitors may join at any stage.

The route leaves Helsingborg through the green fields of Skåne and continues along the irregular coastline of Småland and Östergötland. Excursions can be made to the strange limestone islands of Öland and Gotland, with their interesting folklore and customs. The route then crosses the dense forests of the interior, where there are so many lakes that one is inclined to agree with the old Swedish saying that in Sweden God forgot to divide the land from the water. The route goes close to the Norwegian border, and then returns to Helsingborg along the Kattegat coast, with its many fjords and bays.

Also included in the tour are the great cities of Malmö, Stockholm and Göteborg, the historical towns of Lund, Norrköping and Uppsala, and more than 75 per cent of Sweden's seaside and lakeside resorts.

It is difficult to pinpoint the best parts of this tour, for such things are a matter of individual taste. One visitor will be

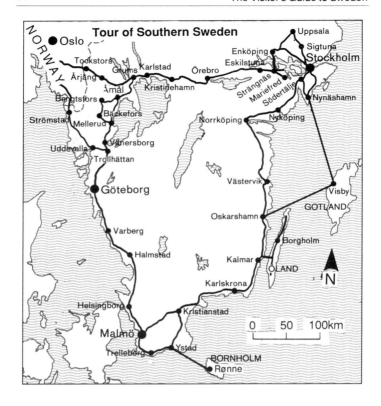

captivated by an old village church, another by the vast,
impenetrable forests, and yet another by a glimpse of an elk. The
angler will be looking for the salmon of his dreams, while the
swimmer will look forward to a morning bathe in one of the lakes or
off some lonely beach. Others will prefer the clean affluence of
the cities, with their many historic buildings, or the fascinating
Stone Age remains.

   Variety is the watchword, and the visitor may choose either
the life of the towns or the solitary peace of the countryside,
much of which has remained untouched by human intervention.
Campers, for example, may prefer the ample facilities of the many
well-organised camping sites, or may opt for the solitary beauty
of the bank of some outlying river or lake.

The lakeland region of Småland

Transport Connections

There are several ways of travelling to Sweden. The direct sea route from Britain is from Newcastle or Felixstowe to Göteborg (25 and 26^1/2 hours). Some travellers may prefer to travel to Dutch, German or Danish ports, continuing overland and taking a ferry from Denmark to Sweden. The shortest crossing from Denmark to Sweden is the ferry from Helsingør to Helsingborg (25 minutes). There are air services to Stockholm and Göteborg. (For more details see page 168 onwards.)

A tour of southern Sweden can be combined with a Norwegian holiday (see *The Visitor's Guide to Norway*). Sections of the route may also be used to reach central and northern Sweden or as part of a journey to Finland (see *The Visitor's Guide to Finland*)

Length and Timing

The overall length of the route is about 1,700km. Taking into account the amount of time required to get to Sweden, one should probably allow at least a fortnight in all. Those wishing to travel overland via Germany and Denmark should allow longer. Depending on the frequency and length of any stops *en route*, one could easily require 3 weeks or more altogether.

Malmöhus Castle, Malmö

The Best Time to Travel
Any time between mid-May and mid-September is suitable for visiting southern Sweden. The bathing season is from late June to early September on the sea coast, but by the lakes it finishes a little sooner, while on the islands of Gotland it often lasts well into September. The southern coastal provinces of Skåne and Blekinge are particularly beautiful during the blossom season, but otherwise the best time to travel is from mid-June to late August. There is not usually any problem of overcrowding — provided, of course, that one avoids a beach near Stockholm on a hot Saturday in July!

The Route
Helsing-
borg

Helsingborg (population 100,000) lies at the narrowest point of the Sound (Öresund), opposite the Danish port of Helsingør. At the time when it belonged to Denmark, Helsingborg was an important garrison town. The Sound was fiercely guarded from both sides, and a toll was demanded from every ship that passed into or out of the Baltic. When Skåne was handed over to Sweden, Helsingborg dwindled in importance, and the port did not grow

Sightseeing in Malmö

again until relatively recently. The town is dominated by a massive tenth-century tower called the Kärnan. It is 35m high and 60m in diameter, with walls more than 4m thick. From the battlements there is a marvellous view over the town and across the Sound to Helsingør (more familiar in English as Hamlet's Elsinore) and the green roofs of the mighty Kronenborg Castle.

The route leaves Helsingborg on the E6 motorway for Malmö, running southwards along the Sound, past the Swedish island of Ven, with Ibb Castle. The first town is **Landskrona** (population 39,000). This lively industrial port is beautifully situated by the Sound. The battlements of the sixteenth-century citadel afford a magnificent view across the Sound to Copenhagen. Selma Lagerlöf was a teacher in Landskrona from 1885 to 1897, and it was during this period that she wrote her novel *Gösta Berling*.

The E6 motorway continues southwards, and about 60km after Helsingborg it arrives at **Malmö** (population 253,000). Malmö is the third-largest town in Sweden and the capital of the province of Skåne. The old town centre is surrounded by canals, and clearly shows the influence of the Danes. In the main market place (Stortorget) is a statue of Carl X Gustav, who won Skåne back from Denmark. The square is surrounded by old buildings, of which the most interesting is the town hall, built in 1546. Behind

22km
Lands-
krona

40km
Malmö

Lund Cathedral

✱ the town hall is St Peter's Church. This fourteenth-century Gothic brick church is the second-largest in Sweden. It possesses a number of Gothic frescos and a magnificent Baroque altar. West of the town centre in the Kungspark (King's Park) is Malmöhus Castle, which was built in the fifteenth and sixteenth centuries during the time of Danish rule. It is now a museum showing the history of Malmö and Skåne. The modern theatre is also worth visiting. Built in 1944, it seats 1,700 people and is the possibly the finest in the whole of Scandinavia.

Excursion to Lund

Malmö
to
Lund
16km
there
and
back

The lovely old university town of **Lund** (population 75,000) is only 8km from Malmö along the R15/E66, which is of motorway standard. It was an important market town as early as AD1000. The famous Romanesque cathedral was begun in 1080, and is probably the finest in Northern Europe. The beautifully formed nave is particularly impressive, as are the richly carved font and

✱ the great fourteenth-century astronomical clock, with its moving figures and chimes. The university was founded in 1660, and is the oldest in Sweden except for Uppsala.

Arboga

A colourful fishing village in Bohuslän

Göteborg

A further 12km out of Lund, through the Dalby Hage National ⌘
Park, is the village of Dalby, which possesses the oldest
surviving church in Sweden, built in 1060.

The route continues southwards from **Malmö** along the E6   Malmö
towards Trelleborg. It passes through a landscape of open
cornfields, reminiscent of the neighbouring country of Denmark. It   16km
comes to a road junction at **Vellinge**.   Vellinge

Excursion to Falsterbo

The L100 road from **Vellinge** offers a nice little excursion to the   Vellinge
twin towns of Skanör and Falsterbo, which are out on the spit of   to
land that marks the southern end of the Sound. Though they are   Falsterbo 32km
now little more than seaside resorts, they were important trading   there
posts at the time of the Hanseatic League. **Falsterbo** has an   and
interesting fourteenth-century church.   back

The E6 continues southwards from **Vellinge**. 10km further on is   Vellinge
the village of Skegri, with an old church and a large grave mound
to the right of the road. The next village of Maglarap also has a
twelfth-century church. The road then runs along the shore   14km
towards Trelleborg.   Trelleborg

The ancient port of **Trelleborg** (population 36,000) used to be
much more important before World War II, when the ferry service
to Sassnitz was the chief traffic route between Sweden and
Germany. But its importance dwindled when Germany was divided
and Sassnitz became part of East Germany. Although a ferry
runs daily to Travemünde in West Germany, most of the traffic
comes up to Sweden via Denmark. Trelleborg was strategically
important in both World Wars. At the end of World War I, the
Germans erected a memorial here not far from where the ferry
docks. This was to thank the Swedes for their help in bringing
prisoners of war out of Russia.

The route continues eastward along the R10 towards Ystad,
running close to the sea shore. It passes through several fishing
villages which have now become popular seaside resorts, and
most of which have fine sandy beaches.   46km
Ystad (population 24,000) is another lovely old town, which   Ystad
again has a Danish look about it. Its medieval buildings cluster
round the old market place, next to which are the historic town hall

Glimmingehus Castle, near Borrby

cellar and St Mary's Church. The church was built in the thirteenth century, but the tower was added later. Further away from the sea is St Peter's Church, which is equally as old. One of the oldest buildings of all is a Franciscan friary called the Gråbrödrakloster (Grey Brothers' Friary), which was built in 1267. The old chapter house and refectory contain some interesting historical exhibits.

Excursion to Bornholm Island
There are several ferries a day from Ystad to Rønne on the Danish island of **Bornholm**; the crossing takes 2¹/₂ hours. There is also a daily ferry service from Simrishamn to Allinge. One possibility is to go out from Ystad and return from Allinge to Simrishamn, missing out the south-eastern corner of Skåne. Although the island is much closer to Sweden (only 40km), it has belonged to Denmark since the sixteenth century. It is one of the most interesting parts of Scandinavia, and should be included in the itinerary if at all possible. Bornholm enjoys good internal transport services, so it is not essential to take a car. The island possesses a rich cultural heritage, and is popular with holiday-makers.

The R10 continues from **Ystad** through gently undulating   Ystad
countryside with fields and orchards. Numerous side-roads lead
off to the small seaside resorts along the Baltic coast. Of these,
Kåseberga is probably the most interesting. On the brow of a hill   ⌘
is an ancient grave site that goes back to the fourth century AD.
It is built out of blocks of stone in the shape of a ship.
                                                                      32km
Half-way to Simrishamn is the village of **Borrby**. A few   Borrby
kilometres beyond Borrby, a small road goes off to the fifteenth-   ⌘
century castle of Glimmingehus. It has been beautifully preserved, and is nowadays used as a restaurant. It is referred to in
Selma Lagerlöf's novel *The Wonderful Journey of Little Nils
Holgersson*. The R10 goes on past several villages and farms to   34km
the ancient port of **Simrishamn**, with its twelfth-century church.   Simris-
There is a daily ferry service from here to **Bornholm** (see   hamn
above).

The R10 turns northward along the coast, passing through the
small resorts of Baskemölla and Vik to the old fishing village of
Kivik, which is also a popular seaside resort. The nearby Kivik   Kivik
Monument is a reconstruction of a Bronze Age tomb. The   ⌘
surrounding countryside is undulating and covered with orchards.
The sea is often hidden by densely wooded hills, which reach a
maximum height of 100m at Kap Stenshuvud just before Kivik.

Shortly after Kivik, the R10 turns inland, and comes into the   9km
R20 near **Brösarp**. The route joins the R20, going via Maglehem   Brösarp
to **Olseröd**, where there is a right turn for Åhus (just past the   11km
level crossing). The route stays with the R20 as it runs through a   Olseröd
park-like landscape with orchards and copses. Skåne is
peppered with castles and manor houses, and is thus reminiscent
of the Loire region of France. After passing Everöd and Lyngsjö,   20km
the R20 comes into the R15/E66 at **Nöbbelöv**. Just before this   Nöbbelöv
junction, there is an interesting twelfth-century church on the
right, behind which is Kristianstad airport.

From here it is only a short distance along the R15/E66 to
Kristianstad (population 55,000), which is situated at the point   12km
where the Helgaå (å = river, brook) runs into Hammersjön (sjö =   Kristiansta
lake). It is a modern industrial town with a technical college. It was
founded in 1614 to serve as a garrison town for Christian IV of
Denmark. Although little of the fortress remains, the streets in the
town centre still retain the grid pattern that was typical of the
period. Across the river are the ruins of Lillöhus Castle, which is   ⌘
older than the town and goes back to the fifteenth century. The
former parade ground, now the Stora torg (Great Market Square),

is surrounded by interesting buildings.

⌘ Trinity Church is as old as the town itself. It is built of brick in the Danish Renaissance style, which was again typical of the period. Also of interest is the old Garvaregården (Tanner's Workshop) in Tivoligatan, which goes back to the seventeenth century. This has now been turned into a restaurant. Between the town centre and the Helgaå is Tivoli Park — a typically Scandinavian park, with restaurants, museums and sports facilities. There are several interesting castles and churches in the area, and the nearby port of Åhus is also worth a visit.

From Kristianstad the route follows the E66, which is a particularly good road at this stage. After 8km the L118 comes in from Åhus (see above). After another 6km there is a turning on ⌘ the right for **Trolle Ljungby** — one of the largest and richest estates in the country, with a seventeenth-century castle. The E66 passes Ivosjön on the left, and leaves the green and populous province of Skåne for Blekinge, with its many lakes and

48km
Sölves-
borg

its rocky coastline.

The next town is **Sölvesborg** (population 15,000) — an old seaport with a ruined castle. 5km further on, at the village of Ysane, is a twelfth-century church with beautiful medieval wall

10km
Gammels-
torp

paintings. The E66 crosses a rocky peninsula and returns to the shore at Gammelstorp. From here onwards the coast is notice-

King's Cottage, Åhus

Trolle Ljungby
Castle

ably more rocky and bare. The road continues along the shore, and after 10km passes **Pukavik** on the left, where the twelfth-century church contains some lovely medieval frescos. The E66 is of motorway standard from Pukavik up to just beyond Ronneby, and the slip roads are the only exits. The second exit is for **Karlshamn** (population 31,000), where the harbour is guarded by the island fortification of Kastelholmen.

22km
Karls-
hamn

The road continues through a rocky, undulating landscape, from which the sea is rarely visible. Just after Åryd, a side-road goes down to the coast, where it passes a number of beaches and camping sites, returning to the E66 at Ronneby. The popular spa town of **Ronneby** (population 30,000) is situated at the point where the Ronnebyå enters the Ronnebyfjord. The famous iron-bearing springs of Ronnebybrunn are 2km further south towards the sea.

32km
Ronneby

Soon after Ronneby, a warning sign indicates that the road is now entering the Karlskrona military zone (*skyddsområde*), which goes almost as far as Kristianopel, well to the other side of Karlskrona. Visitors should keep to the roads, and observe the strict regulations that apply to foreigners (see page 192). Just after Forklära there is a right turn for Hjörtahammar, which is the site of a huge Iron Age burial site. The E66 continues to Nättraby, with its twelfth-century church, and eventually comes to the junction for Karlskrona.

The military town of **Karlskrona** (population 65,000) lies just off the Baltic coast. It is distributed over thirty islands, most of which are connected by bridges. Its magnificent natural harbour is of great strategic importance. The old town is clustered round the Stora torg (Great Market Square), and goes back to 1680, the year when the town was founded. The Shipping Museum is also interesting. The old dockyard includes a fascinating collection of ships' figureheads and an old wooden church. Foreign visitors must get permission from the guards, but this is usually no problem.

Outside Karlskrona the special military regulations must be strictly observed. The route continues along the R15/E66 through

25km
Karls-
krona

Hagby's round church

Fine old belfry, Hagby

the military zone. The road passes the ruined castle of Lyckeby, and enters a rather bare landscape with one or two scattered hamlets. About 5km after Jämjö the road leaves the military zone and arrives at **Fågelmara**. Soon after that there is a right turn along a side-road for Kristianopel (7km), an old coastal fortification. Then there is a left turn for the village of Brömsebro, which was important in the Danish–Swedish peace treaties of 1541 and 1645.

35km
Fågelmara

The E66 now leaves Blekinge for the province of Småland as it continues along the coast. At first the road is some distance from the sea, but later it comes closer, providing some marvellous views across Kalmar Sound to the island of Öland, which runs parallel to the coast for many miles. The road passes the village of Bergkvara to the right. Further on there is a right turn for **Hagby**, just off the E66; Hagby has a fascinating twelfth-century Romanesque round church. Similar round churches are to be found elsewhere in Scandinavia — on Bornholm Island, for example.

36km
Hagby
⌘

The E66/R15 stays close to the coast, and soon arrives at

24km
Kalmar

Kalmar (population 45,000). Kalmar lies at the narrowest point of the Kalmar Sound, and was the most important ferry port for Öland until the building of the Öland Bridge. It is a town steeped in history. The Treaty of Kalmar was signed here in 1397, bringing Norway, Sweden and Denmark together under the Danish crown. The old city is on the island of Kvarnholmen, which can be reached via a bridge from the newer suburbs. It is centred round the Stora torg (Great Market Square). Next to it are the seventeenth-century cathedral and the old town hall, plus the more modern structure of the new town hall. Past the old town hall to the south of the Stora torg is the famous seventeenth-century Kavaljer Gate. Further on is the Lilla torg (Little Market Square), which is again surrounded by fine seventeenth-century buildings such as the Provost's House (Domprostgården), the Governor's Residence (Länsresidenset) and the Sailors' House (Sjömanshuset).

A bridge past the railway station leads back to the mainland. A left turn through the municipal park leads quickly to Kalmar Castle. This massive five-towered structure goes back to the twelfth century, but most of it was built in the sixteenth and seventeenth centuries. The castle is open to the public, and a visit is highly recommended, providing a vivid impression of Swedish culture during the Renaissance, which was Sweden's golden age. The chapel and the King's Chamber (Kungsmaket) are of particular interest.

Old windmills, Öland

The sandy beach of Öland

Tour of the Island of Öland

The island of Öland can be reached from Kalmar via Europe's longest bridge. It is Sweden's second-largest island and also its smallest province. The island is more than 140km long, but measures only 16km at its widest point; it lies parallel to the south-eastern coast of Sweden like an enormous Viking longboat.

The island consists of a vast limestone plateau, which forms steep cliffs along its western shore. The coastal areas are covered with fields and orchards, and peppered with numerous windmills. The interior of the island consists of a bare steppeland known as the Stora Alvar, which is covered with shrubs and rare plants that form a colourful carpet of flowers in the spring. The north is more wooded and has a rich variety of birds.

The island has been inhabited since prehistoric times, as is shown by its 4,000-year-old Stone Age graves near Resmo. A fifth-century village has been reconstructed at Eketorp, while Viking remains include the Karlevisten runestone. Öland is famous for its windmills. Of the original 2,000 only 400 remain, most of them protected as national monuments.

Solliden, summer residence of the royal family

Thanks to its warm summer climate, Öland has become a popular holiday island. Its twenty-five camping sites are full of tourists who come to make cycle tours around the island. The Swedish royal family have their summer residence at Solliden near Borgholm.

Suggested Route (about 350km)
Öland Bridge • Färjestaden • Resmo • Ottenby • Eketorp • Långlöt • Föra • Sandvik • Byerums • Byxelkrok • Grankullavik • Böda • Borgholm • Öland Bridge

The Öland Bridge crosses the Kalmar Sound and forms the road route to the island. Built in 1972, it is the longest bridge in Europe. It is 6km long and supported on 153 pillars. 90,000cu m concrete and 6,000 tonnes of steel were required to build it.

At the end of the bridge there is a zoo to the left and the island's main tourist centre to the right. This modern building is of generous proportions. It is full of models and charts giving information about the island's fauna, flora, geology and history. Maps, plans and brochures are available in many different languages.

The route turns south via **Färjestaden** to the first of Öland's historical monuments. The **Karlevisten** runestone was inscribed during the Viking period in the tenth century AD and honours a Danish prince. The stone stands in the middle of a field to the right of the road.

A short way further on is the village of **Resmo**, where there is a twelfth-century church containing some fine frescos. There is a Bronze Age grave mound and a Stone Age cemetery at nearby Mysinge.

The **Stora Alvar** opens out to the left of the road. This arid plateau is typical of Öland and forms mirages in hot weather. In the spring it is covered with a colourful variety of flowers. The area supports a number of rare plant and bird species.

The **Ottenby** area at the southern end of the island has also been turned into a nature reserve. The road passes through the **Kungsgård**. a wooded area with fallow and roe deer. The whole of this southern part of the island is enclosed by the famous **Karl X Gustav Wall**, built in 1650 to keep the deer inside the royal game reserve. At the southernmost point is Sweden's tallest lighthouse, the **Långe Jan**.

The route turns north again along the east coast of the island. The next place of interest is **Eketorp**, a reconstructed village with a castle showing how people lived in the fifth century AD. The road continues via the attractive little village of **Gräsgård**, the 2km long cemetery at **Seby**, with its 200 gravestones and the **Segerstad** runestone.

The landscape becomes more varied as the road runs up the coast. The medieval church at **Långlöt** contains some lovely frescos and is surrounded by its original graveyard. At **Lerkaka** there are five typical Öland windmills. 2km to the north is the **Himmelberga Museum**, made up of old farmhouses with interiors restored to their original form.

Gärdslösa has another medieval church with frescos. 6km to the west is an ancient cemetery with a stone formation in the shape of a boat. There are yet more windmills along the road to the north.

At **Föra** the route enters the main L136 road, which it follows north as far as **Södvik**. Then there is a left turn along a side road to **Sandvik**, which is back on the west coast of the island. Its chief attraction is the great **Dutch Windmill**, built in 1885, with its enormous wooden gearwheels. A small unmade road goes along the coast to the old whetstone mill of **Jordhamn**.

The route returns to the L136 and carries on northwards as far as **Högby** where it turns left again to the coast at **Byerums**. The

Gärdslösa Church

 coast from Sandvik to Byerums is characterised by strange *raukar* formations where the limestone has been eroded into wierd shapes.

The next place is the small fishing port and tourist resort of **Byxelkrok** which is surrounded by thick birch forest. There are ferries from here to Oskarshamn on the mainland and to the nearby island of **Blå jungfrun** ('The Blue Maiden') which is a bird colony and a nature reserve.

The route continues around the northen tip of the island past the **Neptuni åkrar** ('Gardens of Neptune'), an area of boulders with blue flowers growing among them. Nearby is the small port of **Grankullavik-Nabbelund**, from which there is a summer ferry service to Visby on the island of Gotland. Stretching to the south is **Trollskoven**, an ancient pine forest with strange tree formations.

The route comes back to the L136, along which it returns southwards to **Borgholm** (population 2,500). Borgholm is the island's main village and commercial centre and is also the main tourist and seaside resort. Its castle was built in the sixteenth century on the site of a thirteenth-century fort. It was burned down in 1806 and now lies in ruins. At Solliden to the south is the summer residence of the Swedish royal family, the grounds of which are sometimes open to the public.

The L136 carries on southwards through oak woodlands that mostly hide the coast. It eventually reaches the small village of **Algutsrum** and the zoo by the Öland Bridge where the tour began.

The R15/E66 continues due north from Kalmar, and keeps fairly close to the coast. The landscape varies between woods and fields, and the villages are mostly very small. If there is time to spare, one can turn off the E66 at Kåremo and take a small road along the rocky coastline. The coast road goes through Timmernabben, and comes back into the E66/R15 just before **Mönsterås** (population 13,000) — a small port with a match factory. The E66 later crosses the Emån — a river which is beloved of anglers for its great numbers of trout and salmon. To the right of the road is the seaside resort of Påskallavik.

The road leaves the coast and arrives at the port of **Oskarshamn** (28,000). Oskarshamn was the birthplace of the doctor, writer and archaeologist Axel Munthe, who wrote *The Story of San Michele*. The sculptor Axel Petersson (1868–1925) was also born here, and some of his works are on show at the local museum. There is a summer boat service from Oskarshamn to the island of Blå Jungfrun, which is a nature reserve. There are also ferries during the summer to Byxelkrok on Öland and Visby on Gotland.

Kalmar

45km
Mönsterås

31km
Oskars-
hamn

Excursion to Gotland and a Tour of the Island
There are three ferry routes to Visby from the Swedish mainland: from Oskarshamn (see above), from Västervik (see page 81) and from Nynäshamn (south of Stockholm). There is also a ferry to Visby from Grankullavik on Öland (see page 76). It is possible to combine two ferry routes. One might, for example, arrive from Oskarshamn and leave on the ferry to Nynäshamn, continuing north to Stockholm (see page 84). Visitors who return via the same ferry route may not need to take a car across, since much of the island is accessible by public transport. Those staying longer, however, are advised to bring a car with them. The island is ideal for cycling tours.

Gotland lies out in the Baltic, 90km from the Swedish coast. The island has an area of 3,200sq km and a population of 56,000. Like Öland, it consists of a limestone plateau, and its geology and

Russian ponies, Gotland

landscape are quite different from those of the mainland. The results of cave explorations show that the island has been inhabited for more than 7,000 years. It possesses a rich archaeological heritage from all periods of Swedish history, much of which is on display at the Museum of Antiquities in Visby. The island is intensively cultivated, thanks to its fertile soils and favourable climate.

The northern part of Gotland is a restricted military zone (*skyddsområde* — see page 192), so the suggested tour has been limited to the central and southern parts of the island. Visitors with limited time are recommended to see Visby, Roma and Dalhem, all of which are easily accessible by public transport.

The history of Gotland is closely bound up with the Hanseatic League, and thus with the cities of north Germany. The island had originally been colonised by the Goths, who had long since had trade links with Russia via Novgorod. These were expanded to include the Hansa merchants. At the end of the thirteenth century the merchants of Visby and Lübeck formed an alliance to defend the Baltic against piracy. Visby and Gotland were several times conquered by the Danes, but the island continued to prosper until the middle of the fourteenth century. The island possesses as many as 100 churches from the Hansa period. Gotland has belonged to Sweden since 1645.

There are a number of unusual phenomena on the island. The *raukar*, for example, are wierdly shaped columns of rock that have been sculpted out of the limestone by the waves. The lush meadows of Gotland contain many interesting species of wild orchid. The bird life on the coast includes a large number of auk species, while the heaths and woodlands of the interior are the habitat of a rare breed of pony that is unique to the island. It is between 120cm and 140cm high, and has two toes instead of a hoof. The islanders call it the Russian Pony, because it is supposed to have been brought over to Europe by Attila the Hun, 1,500 years ago.

Visby (population 21,000) is the obvious starting point for a Visby tour of the island. Although the town was so often attacked and destroyed, it has managed to preserve its medieval atmosphere.

Visby

Lärbro Church, Gotland

This is largely thanks to the fact that the old city walls have remained mostly intact. They were built out of limestone in the twelfth century; they are about 4,000m long, and are still guarded by thirty-eight towers.

Visitors should take a stroll along Strandgatan, the main street, which has some lovely old buildings. There is, for example, the Burmeisterskahus (the house of Burmeister, a merchant from Lübeck), which now houses the tourist information office. Further along are the Museum of Antiquities and many more old houses with their typical crow-stepped gables. Next to the main market square (Stora torg) are the remains of the old Gothic church of St Catherine. There are several more ruined churches, of which Drotten (Trinity) and St Lars are not far away. They are the remnants of seventeen churches, of which only the cathedral is still in use. St Mary's Cathedral was built in the twelfth century by the merchants of Lübeck. These are only a few of the many interesting things to be found in Visby.

The suggested route goes south-westwards from Visby along

the L143 to **Roma**, which has a twelfth-century church. Just outside the village are the ruins of a Cistercian monastery, built in 1164. Only 5km away at Barlingho is another lovely thirteenth-century church with a beautiful twelfth-century font. The route continues south-west along the L145. At Västerby there is a side-turning into the woods towards the prehistoric fortifications of Torsburgen and Herrgårdsklint. 8km further on, the L145 arrives at **Ljugarn** — a pretty seaside resort, with a sandy beach that faces out across the Baltic.

20km
Roma

28km
Ljugarn

The route turns south-east along the L144, and after 7km arrives at **Alskog**, which has an eleventh-century church. Nearby are some Bronze Age stone monuments in the form of ships. The L144 goes on via Garde to Lye, where it joins the L143 via Stånge to **Hemse**. All these villages have ancient medieval churches. From Hemse, the L142 goes due south via Havdhem to Fidernäs, where it joins the west coast of the island as far as **Burgsvik**.

28km
Hemse

25km
Burgsvik

From Burgsvik a small road goes east towards the lovely old village of **Öja**, where the thirteenth-century church contains a beautiful Burgundian crucifix from the same period. The route turns northward again, through the old village of Fide, with yet another thirteenth-century church. It then returns to Fidernäs, and continues northwards along the L140 to **Klintehamn**. From Klintehamn there is a motor-launch service to the bird island of Stora Karlsö, which is a nature reserve. Special permission is needed to visit the island, for which inquiries should be made at the tourist office in Visby.

45km
Klinte-
hamn

The L140 carries on northwards via Västergarn and Tofta, both of which have lovely medieval churches. At Tofta there is also a sea-bathing station. From here it is only a short distance to **Visby**.

34km
Visby

Soon after **Oskarshamn**, the E66 turns away from the coast, which becomes more and more irregular. The road runs through mostly flat country between lakes and fjords, crossing the Gunnebo Bridge, until it arrives at the turning for **Västervik** (population 43,000). The lovely old port of Västervik is gorgeously situated among the inlets and skerries of the coast. The town centre is full of old wooden houses, with the beautiful fifteenth-century church of St Gertrude. There is a summer ferry service from Västervik to Visby on Gotland (see page 77).

Oskars-
hamn

84km
Väst-
ervik

Nyköpingshus Castle

The E66 continues to Almvik, where it meets Gamlebyviken —
a fjord over 20km long, which is a real angler's paradise. At the
top of the fjord is the small town of **Gamleby** (population 6,000).
The road now enters a region that is truly typical of Sweden, with
its woods and meadows, and its innumerable lakes. It sometimes
passes fjords that are indistinguishable from lakes. Just before
Valdemarsvik, the road leaves Småland and enters the province
of Östergötland. **Valdemarsvik** is a small town at the top end of
Valdemarsviken — a fjord which is again 20km long and full of
fish.

19km
Gamleby

45km
Valde-
marsvik

The E66 continues through the gently undulating landscape of
Östergötland, with its meadows, woods and lakes. The town of
Söderköping (10,000) is situated near the eastern end of the
Göta Canal (see page 161), which runs right through the heart of
Sweden. The canal links the two cities of Göteborg and
Stockholm, and provides a trade route between the northern
Baltic Sea and the Skagerrak. It is more than 100 years old, and
mostly makes use of natural waterways such as rivers and lakes.
20km east of Söderköping is the vast ruin of Stegeborg Castle,
which was built in the sixteenth century at the time of Gustav
Vasa.

40km
Söder-
köping

16km further on, the E66 comes to an end at the industrial port of **Norrköping** (population 120,000 — see page 110). Norr- köping is situated at the end of a long inlet called Bråviken at the point where the River Motala comes in. The river once formed an impressive torrent through the centre of the town, but since the water has been harnessed for electricity, it has been reduced to no more than a stream. To the north of the town is **Kolmården Safari Park**. 6km north-west of the town towards Svärtinge is the Ringstad estate, which includes the remains of a seventh-century Viking fortification and an extensive burial site.

16km
Norr-
köping

The route leaves Norrköping in a north-easterly direction along the busy E4, which forms the main artery between Göteborg and Stockholm. It runs through gently undulating green countryside, which is continually interspersed by lakes and rivers. After Örsted the road leaves Östergötland for the province of Södermanland, which is covered with lakes.

The route comes close to the coast again at **Nyköping** (population 62,000). Nyköping is a modern industrial town, but was also very important during the Middle Ages. Nyköpingshus Castle was originally built in the thirteenth century, but was rebuilt in its present form following a fire in 1665. Nyköping was the meeting place for the parliament on fifteen occasions during the Middle Ages. The L217 goes from Nyköping to **Oxelösund**, which forms the centre of a popular holiday area among the skerries on the coast. It is also the site of the largest steelworks in Sweden.

63km
Nyköp-
ing

The E4 goes on towards Stockholm through gently undulating country, whose woods, meadows and lakes give it a park-like appearance. There are warning signs on the roadside, showing a black animal on a yellow background. These indicate the points where elk cross the road. They must be taken seriously, since a collision with such a large beast will prove dangerous for both parties. About 40km after Nyköping, where the E4 by-passes **Vagnhärad**, there is a turning off along the L218 for the popular seaside resort of **Trosa**. Trosa lies in a bay full of islands and skerries, providing marvellous opportunities for camping. Just south of Trosa, a bridge goes across to the island of Öbolandet, the southern half of which is occupied by a camping site, which has all the necessary facilities laid on.

40km
Vagn-
härad

The E4 turns northwards, and often meets one of the many Baltic fjords, which come a long way inland along this part of the coast. The road soon arrives at **Södertälje** (population 78,000) — a modern industrial town, which is the home of large firms such

35km
Söder-
tälje

Steninge Castle

as Saab-Scania. The town is situated on the banks of Lake Mälaren at the point where it is linked to the Baltic via a short canal. Lake Mälaren is a large and irregularly-shaped lake, full of small islands. Södertälje is famous for its open-air museum at Torekällberg. There is an animal enclosure and a 'Wild West' display of cowboys on horses.

Detour via Nynäshamn
(97km Södertälje to Stockholm)

Just past where the E4 crosses the canal at Södertälje, there is a turning along the L225 for Nynäshamn. This road goes south through delightful green countryside as far as Ösmo, where it meets the L73 coming from Stockholm. A few kilometres further south is **Nynäshamn** (population 8,000). Nynäshamn is a popular beach resort for the people of Stockholm, and should therefore be avoided at weekends during the summer. It is also a ferry port, with services to Visby on the island of Gotland (see page 77). Travellers who have come over to Nynäshamn from Gotland should join the route at this point. The L73 leads directly northwards to **Stockholm**.

Söder-
tälje
The E4 continues from **Södertälje** to Stockholm. Though it has

Skokloster Castle, near Sigtuna

been a motorway for some time, it becomes noticeably busier as it approaches the capital. The E4 comes into Stockholm along Södertäljevägen, crossing other roads in vast cloverleaf junctions, where the stranger can easily get lost. The best way to avoid this is to follow the signs for Staden. These eventually lead to the Royal Palace in the heart of the city, where one can park the car in one of the large car parks by the harbour. For full details about **Stockholm**, see page 37.

35km
Stock-
holm

Detour via Sigtuna and Uppsala
(113km Stockholm to Enköping)
The E4 motorway leaves **Stockholm** in a northerly direction. Just past the village of Norrviken, it passes the lovely twelfth-century church of Sollentuna on the left. At Märsta there is a left turn onto the L263, which leads to Sigtuna.

Stock-
holm

Sigtuna (population 4,000) is one of the oldest towns in Sweden. In the eleventh century it was the capital of Sweden and an important centre for trade. In 1187 it was destroyed by invaders from Estonia. It is not known how big the old city was, but the ruins of the tenth- and eleventh-century churches of St Olof, St Per and St Lars bear witness to the extent of its former glory. The lovely eighteenth-century building in the market place

35km
Sigtuna
⌘

Uppsala Cathedral

is the smallest town hall in Sweden. The main street is also very picturesque. St Mary's Church is pure Gothic in style. It was built in the thirteenth century next to the ruins of St Olof's. Also worth seeing is the fine Gothic chapel in the cemetery opposite the church.

One place worth visiting if time allows is **Skokloster Castle**, which can be reached from Sigtuna via Erikssund and Häggeby, or otherwise by boat. Also in the same area are the manor houses of Rosersberg, Steninge and Venngarn, parts of which are open to the public. The route continues northwards from Sigtuna via Haga, Vassuda and Sunnersta, passing through a nature reserve along the shores of Lake Ekoln.

35km
Uppsala

The road soon arrives at **Uppsala** (population 130,000) — the home of Sweden's oldest university. The ancient city of Uppsala is without doubt one of the most fascinating cities in Europe. In prehistoric times it was the centre of a religious cult. The Swedes were later converted to Christianity, and in 1164 the archbishopric was moved to Uppsala. The city has remained the religious centre

*Linnaeus Gardens,
Uppsala*

of Sweden. The only part of the old city to have survived is the area immediately below the castle. In a wooden tower next to the castle is Uppsala's famous Gunilla Bell, which rings in the new day at six o'clock each morning, and rings out the old one at nine in the evening.

Uppsala Cathedral is the one of the largest in Scandinavia. It is Gothic in style, and was begun in the twelfth century. The spires were destroyed by fire, but were later rebuilt to a height of 118m. In Odinslund, not far from the castle, is the old Trinity Church, also known as the Peasants' Church. The oldest parts of the building go back to the twelfth century, and are decorated inside with some beautiful medieval wall paintings.

The University Library contains more than two million books and 28,000 manuscripts. Its most valuable possession is Bishop Wulfila's *Silver Bible* — an ancient Gothic version of the four Gospels, written in silver letters on purple parchment. The oldest part of the university is the Gustavianum — a domed building, which was once used for anatomical demonstrations. Linnaeus, the great botanist and taxonomist, worked and taught at Uppsala University. His botanic garden has been restored to its original form, and this, together with the rooms where he worked, has been turned into a museum.

⚘   5km to the north of the city is Gamla Uppsala (Old Uppsala), which in pre-Christian times was the capital of the Svear (see page 28). The old medieval cathedral was built here on the site of the former temple to the god of light. There is now a little stone church on the site, which is built of remnants of the cathedral. The church is surrounded by burial mounds. They are known as Kungshögarna (the Royal Hills), and go back to the fifth and sixth centuries.

The route goes south-west from Uppsala along the L55. The gently undulating countryside is mostly covered with forests. The road passes through several old villages, and eventually comes back into the main route again at Litslena, where it joins the E18 as far as **Enköping.**·

46km
Enköp-
ing

Stock-
holm

The main route leaves **Stockholm** along the E18 motorway in a northerly direction through the suburb of Solna, where it goes close to Karolinska sjukhuset, a large hospital complex. It then divides off from the E4 Uppsala motorway, which goes off to the right. The road keeps to the north of Lake Mälaren, which, being fragmented into fjords and bays, keeps appearing and disappearing. The next town is **Enköping** (population 14,500), which was an important medieval town, though virtually nothing remains from that period.

80km
Enköp-
ing

⚘   Just beyond Enköping, the route turns south along the L55. The road crosses Lake Mälaren via a beautiful stretch of islands and waterways, which it negotiates by means of bridges and causeways. Immediately south of Lake Mälaren is the small town of **Strängnäs** (population 8,300), which was once a Viking capital. Strängnäs has been a bishopric since the twelfth century, and the thirteenth-century cathedral bears witness to its former glory.

30km
Sträng-
näs

Excursion to Mariefred and Gripsholm Castle

Sträng-
näs to
Marie-
fred
40km
there
and
back
⚘

Mariefred is to the south-east of Strängnäs along the E3 to Södertälje. After 18km there is a left turn for the small town of Mariefred. **Mariefred** is famous for its railway museum, and in particular for **Gripsholm Castle** (see page 111), which is a jewel among castles. The author and journalist Kurt Tucholsky, who died in 1936, is buried in the cemetery here. The return route is back along the E3 to Strängnäs

The main route turns right at **Strängnäs** along the E3. This road runs westward alongside a branch of Lake Mälaren, then goes inland towards **Eskilstuna** (population 93,000), which it by-passes. Eskilstuna is the home of the Swedish iron and steel industry. Reinhold Rademacher founded twenty forges here in 1658, six of which are still preserved. They have been turned into museums, in which demonstrations are given showing how the art of forging has changed down the centuries. These form part of the open-air museum site, which is situated next to the largest zoo in Sweden. Sträng-näs 33km Eskils-tuna

The E3 continues through dense forests close to the shores of Lake Mälaren, which remains mostly invisible from the road. The next town is **Kungsör** (population 7,000), which is situated at the point where the Arbogaån runs into Lake Mälaren. 12km further on, the road crosses the Hjälmar Canal, which links Lake Hjälmaren with Lake Mälaren. This is closely followed by the town of **Arboga** (population 12,000), whose former importance is shown by the medieval half-timbered buildings in the town centre and the twelfth-century stone church. 30km Kungsör 16km Arboga ⚯

The E3 is still a good, fast road as it leaves the old ironworking province of Västmanland for the endless forests of Närke. Every now and then an old church peeps out from a clearing in the trees. The road soon arrives at the modern town of **Örebro** (population 120,000), which is the provincial capital of Närke. Örebro lies on the Svartån in a beautiful setting at the western end of Lake Hjälmaren. On an island in the river is Örebro Castle — an old Renaissance building. There are some Iron Age burial sites not far away. 43km Örebro ⚯

The route now leaves the E3 (which turns southwards) and continues westwards along the E18. Not far from Örebro, the route crosses a provincial boundary into Värmland, thereby entering the lovely green province of Selma Lagerlöf's novel *Gosta Berling*. The road crosses a range of wooded hills called the Kilsberge. It then runs along the north shore of Lake Möckeln past the famous Bofors steelworks to **Karlskoga** (population 39,000). 46km Karls-koga

The route continues westwards through deep forests until it arrives at **Kristinehamn** (population 28,000), where it joins route 4 as far as Karlstad (see page 126). Kristinehamn is situated at the north-east corner of **Lake Vänern**, which with an area of 5,546sq km is by far the biggest lake in Sweden. The town has a growing industrial base, and serves as a port for the trans- 27km Kristine-hamn

*Picasso's
sculpture
Kristinehamn*

shipment of iron and timber from the hinterland. Lake Vänern is linked via the Göta Canal to both the Baltic and the Skagerrak (see page 161). The townspeople are proud of the 15m high Picasso sculpture which stands by the lake shore in front of the town. It was personally donated by the artist himself.

The E18 continues close to the northern shore of Lake Vänern through a land of rivers and forests, with only occasional glimpses of the lake. It does not meet the shore proper until just before **Karlstad** (population 52,000), which is beautifully situated by the lake. Karlstad has been important since the Middle Ages. The old town was built of wood, and most of it was destroyed in the great fire of 1865. However, a few of the old houses have survived in Älvgatan — the road along the bank of the Klarälv, which flows through the town. Karlstad is the provincial capital of Värmland, and the home of several large wood-processing firms. The E18 continues westwards to **Grums**. At a road junction after Grums, the R45 turns southwards towards Vänersborg, while the E18 goes on towards the Norwegian border.

71km
Karlstad

26km
Grums

Detour into Norway via Oslo
(459km Grums to Vänersborg)

Grums

This route stays on the E18 after **Grums**, passing through dense forests interspersed by rivers and lakes. It goes via Ökne and Sillerud to **Årjäng**. The landscape becomes increasingly hilly as the forests continue towards the Norwegian border. There are no customs formalities, either at the Swedish post at **Hån** or at the Norwegian post at **Ørje**. Customs regulations within Scandinavia have been greatly simplified, and passport and driving licence are the most that might need to be shown. The road carries on, past a long, narrow lake called the Rødenessjø, to **Askim** (population 8,000). Soon after Askim, it crosses the Glomma, which at 600km is the longest river in Scandinavia, and provides Norway with a vast source of energy. The road meets the E6 at Nordby, and approaches the Norwegian capital from the south. **Oslo** (population 480,000) is described in detail in *The Visitor's Guide to Norway*.

81km
Årjäng

30km
Norwegian
border

47km
Askim

53km
Oslo

The route returns southwards from Oslo, but this time stays on the E6. After 30km there is a right turn for the beach resort of Drøbak and Oscarsborg Fort. The E6 continues southwards, keeping close to the Oslofjord, and passes **Hølen** on the right. A short way further on is the port of **Moss** (population 25,000), from which a ferry goes to Horten on the opposite side of the fjord. The E6 now runs parallel to a ridge called the Ryggerød, which during the ice age formed a moraine at the edge of the ice sheet.

68km
Moss

Just before Sarpsborg, the road passes the small village of Tune, with a lovely old eleventh-century church. The area around here is full of prehistoric and Viking settlements, including some of Norway's oldest known archaeological remains. **Sarpsborg** (population 13,500) was founded by Olaf the Holy in the eleventh century. This prosperous little town is important for its wood-processing industries. To the south-west of Sarpsborg is the old fortified town of Fredrikstad, which lies at the mouth of the Glomma. On the edge of Sarpsborg, this same river forms a massive 22m waterfall called the Sarpsfoss (*foss* = waterfall). It has partly been harnessed for a power station, but there is so much water in the river that the falls have lost none of their beauty.

⌘

32km
Sarps-
borg

The E6 continues south-eastwards to where the Iddefjord forms the border between Norway and Sweden. (Just before the border, there is a left turn for Halden and Frederiksten Fort, which was a key point in the struggles between Norway and Sweden. There is a monument to King Carl XII of Sweden, who fell here in 1718.) The E6 crosses the border to **Svinesund** via a 450m long reinforced concrete bridge, which runs 65m above the water.

20km
Swedish
border

Dalsland Canal

17km
Norrs-
hede
27km
Tanums-
hede
☂

30km
Hälle-
vads-
holm

38km
Udde-
valla
31km
Väners-
borg

The E6 continues at some distance from the coast, which is greatly indented. At **Norrshede** there is a turning for the popular camping and seaside resort of Strömstad. The road runs closer to the coast as far as **Tanumshede**, where there is a turning for the beach resort of Grebbestad. There are numerous Bronze Age rock drawings in this area — some not far from the road. The E6 turns inland again, and passes an extremely good camping site on the left at Solängen. It goes on to **Hällevadsholm**, where the L165 comes in from Halden (see above). It carries on via Dingle to **Gläborg**, from which several roads go down to the beach resorts of Hunnebostrand, Gravarne and Lysekil. All of these have camping sites close to the sea. The E6 continues via Munkedal to **Uddevalla** (population 47,000).

At Uddevalla the route leaves the E6, turning due east along the R44, and eventually rejoining the main route near **Vänersborg**.

The main route goes south from **Grums** along the R45. It crosses Grums the Värmlandsnäs — a promontory that sticks out into Lake Vänern. The next towns are **Säffle** (population 19,000), with its 36km paper and cellulose factories, and **Åmål** (population 13,000). Åmål Though Åmål was founded in 1643, very few of its old wooden houses have survived the many fires which destroyed it. They are grouped near to the river bank, and are surrounded by a modern industrial town. Åmål is in the province of Dalsland, which is covered in lakes and forests as far as the Norwegian border, although the southern part is more agricultural. The many lakes are linked to Lake Vänern by the 100-year-old **Dalsland Canal**, which is 260km long and has twenty-nine locks. It is an important route for the transport of timber, and a trip up the canal is a marvellous way of getting to know the lovely and varied scenery of Dalsland. Information on canal trips is available at Åmål and Mellerud (see below).

Detour via Bengtsfors and Bäckefors
(94km Åmål to Mellerud)
This short detour runs through some of the finest lake and forest scenery that Sweden has to offer, and provides some glimpses of how timber is felled and transported. The route leaves the R45 at Åmål along the L164, and runs through undulating country full of Åmål forests and lakes. The section along the shore of Laxsjön to Laxarby is particularly beautiful. There is a right turn along the 39km L172 for the little town of **Bengtsfors**, which is delightfully Bengts- situated among the lakes. The route turns south via Hedange, fors and returns to the L172 near Billingby on the shore of Laxsjön. 13km The road plunges into dense forests. At **Steneby** there is a Steneby turning for Dals-Ed, which goes yet deeper into the forest. But the present route stays with the L172, skirting the shore of Lake 17km Iväg, and eventually arrives at **Bäckefors.** It turns off here Bäcke-
fors along the L166, which returns via forests and lakes to **Mellerud** 25km on the R45. Mellerud

The main route continues south from **Åmål** along the R45, Åmål staying close to the shore of Lake Vänern. Near Köpmannebro it crosses the Dalsland Canal (see above), and runs along a spit of land that is rather like a causeway. It leaves the shore just before **Mellerud** (population 4,000).
46km
    The road turns inland, but returns to the shore of Lake Vänern Mellerud

42km
Väners-
borg as it approaches **Vänersborg** (population 34,000). The town is on a promontory that sticks out into the lake, and is protected to the south by a sixteenth-century moat. There is a fine stretch of parkland that runs in front of the council buildings in the centre. Vänersborg is the capital of the administrative district of Älvborgs län.

14km
Troll-
hättan The R45 continues southwards from Vänersborg to **Troll-hättan** (population 50,000). The once famous Trollhättan Falls have long since disappeared; for the waters of the Götaälv, which at one time fell 35m in the space of 1.5km, have been diverted for electricity production (up to 200,000kW). The raging torrent has thus been reduced. to a mere trickle along the bed of a gorge which the river has taken thousands of years to carve out of the rock. However, on 2 days a week between May and August, the falls are 'switched on' again as vast quantities of water (350cu m/sec) are rediverted along the old river bed. On the 'Waterfall Days' of mid-July, this event is turned into a special festival.

⌘ The R45 stays close to the Götaälv, which has in several places been harnessed for water and electricity — at Lilla Edet and Älvängen, for example. At **Bohus** there is a castle on an island in the middle of the river, which was built in 1310 by King Håkon of Norway. On the opposite bank is the town of Kungälv (see page 129). 70km
Göte-
borg Now it is only a short distance to **Göteborg** (See page 96).

The E6 continues southwards from Göteborg, keeping fairly close to the Kattegat coast. It runs through an open, undulating landscape, with occasional woodlands. The sea is only visible when the road passes a fjord, which happens, for example, at 28km
Kungs-
backa **Kungsbacka** (population 38,000). The road crosses many rivers and streams, which come down from the lakes of Västergötland.

51km
Varberg The next town is the popular seaside resort of **Varberg** ⌘ (population 43,000). West of the town is a thirteenth-century fortress that has been turned into a museum. Its most interesting exhibit is the medieval clothing from the body of a man that was found preserved in the peat bogs nearby. The road continues 28km
Falken-
berg through open fields to **Falkenberg**, where it crosses the Ätran (a salmon river) via an eighteenth-century toll bridge.

The road goes inland through mostly open, undulating countryside, passing a number of old farms and churches. It 39km
Halmstad returns to the coast again at **Halmstad** (population 75,000), which is the capital of the province of Halland. Its castle was

Miniland, Halmstad

built in the sixteenth and seventeenth centuries, while St Nicolas' Church is a fine medieval construction. Also of interest are a Carl Milles sculpture and the Hallandsgård Museum. On the edge of the town is a miniature town, appropriately called Miniland. 5km along the coast is the seaside resort of **Tylösand**, which has one of the finest sandy beaches in Sweden.

The E6 is of motorway standard as it continues through the heavily cultivated region that borders Laholm Bay. The small town of **Laholm** (population 4,000) is full of little streets with brightly painted wooden houses. The town hall has a lovely old mechanical display of a medieval battle, which works twice a day, at noon and at six o'clock in the evening.

22km
Laholm

The road leaves the Kattegat coast again, and returns to it at Ängelholm, which is at the end of a deep inlet called Skälderviken. The road then crosses a promontory called Höganäs, which forms the entrance to Öresund (the Sound). Soon after that, the road arrives at **Helsingborg** — the ferry port for Denmark that was chosen as the starting point for this route.

3 GÖTEBORG

Göteborg — otherwise known in English as Gothenburg — is the second-largest city in Sweden, with a population of 450,000. It is also one of Scandinavia's busiest and most prosperous cities, and probably the best example of a modern Swedish metropolis.

The city was founded in 1621 by King Gustav II Adolf as Sweden's major western port. This was, however, no more than the relocation of a settlement that had existed at the mouth of the Götaälv since prehistoric times, and which had previously been called Lödöse. Its natural harbour and favourable position had made it so important strategically that between the twelfth and sixteenth centuries it had been continually captured, destroyed, rebuilt and renamed by the vying Scandinavian powers.

When Gustav II Adolf built his new city on the islands which now form the centre, he called on the help of Dutch bankers who were keen to gain a foothold in Scandinavia. They naturally employed Dutch builders and architects, whose influence is still plainly to be seen in the bridges and canals of the old city. Hardly anything is left of the original town, which, though no longer subject to wars, was frequently destroyed by fire in the centuries which followed. Most Swedish towns were built of wood at the time, and the need for heating during severe winters increased the risk of a conflagration, which would spread quickly through the narrow streets of the city.

⌘ The oldest building in Göteborg is the **Örgryte Old Church** (Gamle kyrkan), parts of which go back to the thirteenth century. The oldest secular building is the seventeenth-century **Kronhus**. One of the few remaining buildings from the eighteenth century is the former headquarters of the Dutch East India Company — a trading organisation which was particularly powerful in Göteborg. Like the Kronhus it has been preserved as a museum. The Dutch influence was stronger than ever during the nineteenth century, when the present city centre was built. Protected from the sea by the Nya Älvsborg — an island fortress in front of the city — the port flourished as never before,

Älvsborgs Bridge, Göteborg

especially after the building of the Göta Canal, which opened up trade with the Baltic. All that remain of the original city defences are the enclosing moats, a massive tower called **Skansen Kronan** (now a museum), and the **Carolus Tower** in Kungsgatan in the centre of the city.

Göteborg has now become the largest trading port in the whole of Scandinavia. More than 50,000 ships dock here annually, moving more than 20 million tonnes of cargo. Göteborg handles a third of Sweden's exports. It is also an important fishing port, with an annual catch of 25,000 tonnes. The port has attracted a large variety of industries, including the world-famous Volvo car factory, which sells 60 per cent of its vehicles abroad, and the famous SKF ball-bearing factory, which also exports a large proportion of its products. Göteborg has thus become the richest city in Sweden. Several new satellite towns have grown up around it, all of them well supplied with shops and services.

The city has become a popular centre for conferences and exhibitions, and the extensive trade fair centre almost always has something going on. Göteborg is also a good cultural centre, with international opera seasons at the Grand Theatre (Stora teatern), and a concert hall that has some of the best acoustics in the

world. The coastal areas to the north and south of the city are a
paradise for holidaymakers, and especially for yachtsmen. There
are regattas throughout the summer months, including several
international events.

Sightseeing in Göteborg

The city centre within the the old moat defences can be visited on
foot. But those wishing to venture further afield are recommended
to take one of the regular bus sightseeing tours. The rendezvous
point for these tours is in front of the **Grand Theatre**, just over
the moat from the **tourist information office** in Kungsportsavenyn. Maps and information are available in English, and
tours can be arranged with English-speaking guides. There is a
choice of two routes: a tour of the central areas of the city, which
takes only an hour, and a tour of the whole city area. The latter is
much to be recommended, since it incorporates everything that
there is to see, including the new parts of the city and the
Ramberg, from which there is a marvellous panorama of the city.

There are also boat trips in the summer, which depart from the
nearby Kungsportsbron. They run along the old canals and
around the most interesting parts of the harbour.

One of the best places for motorists to park is the Avenyn
multi-storey car park, which is located behind the Domus
department store on Kungsportsavenyn. It is open 24 hours a
day, and access is via Kristinelundsgatan.

City Centre Tour

The best place to start is Götaplatsen — a fine square to the
south-east of the centre at the far end of Kungsportsavenyn. In
the centre of the square is Carl Milles' famous statue of Poseidon,
and surrounding it are the concert hall, the **Museum of Art**, the
City Theatre and the **City Library**.

The route goes into town along Kungsportsavenyn — a fine
boulevard with avenues of lime trees, which is one of the city's
main shopping thoroughfares. It passes the Grand Theatre (see
above), and crosses the moat via Kungsportsbron to
Kungsportsplatsen, where the tourist information office is
located. The route then continues north along Östra Hamngatan,
crossing Kungsgatan, Kyrkogatan and Drottningsgatan — the
three streets which form the city's main shopping centre. They
include a number of interesting shops, and are linked by a

Paddan sightseeing boats, Göteborg

pedestrian precinct called Korsgatan, which is actually heated in winter.

Östra Hamngatan then crosses the main harbour canal (Stora Hamnkanal), which served as the harbour before the building of the modern port. Just across the canal is Gustav Adolf's torg — the square which forms the hub of the old city. It contains a statue of the city's founder, King Gustav II Adolf, and is surrounded by old buildings such as the **Kronhus, East India House** and the old **Stock Exchange**. Not far away along Postgatan are the central station and the main post office. Almost all the old city centre thoroughfares are one-way streets.

The route goes west along the main harbour canal, which is flanked by Norra Hamngatan and Södra Hamngatan. It then turns south along Västra Hamngatan, and crosses back through the shopping centre to the cathedral. **Göteborg Cathedral** was built in the nineteenth century, and is situated on the corner of Västra Hamngatan and Kungsgatan. Also worth visiting in Kungsgatan are **Kristiana's Hunting Lodge**, which is built in the style of the seventeenth century, and **Antikhallarna** — the largest antiques market in Scandinavia.

The route crosses back over the southern moat, and continues along Vasavägen past the university and through Vasa Park to Götaplatsen, where it reaches the starting point again.

Other Things to See in Göteborg

On the eastern side of the city is a broad expanse of parkland, at the northern end of which is the Ullevi Stadium, built for the 1958 World Cup football championships. South of this is the **Scandinavium**, the largest indoor arena in Northern Europe. The trade fair centre is one of the most modern in Sweden, and is the site for many important conferences and exhibitions. Finally, there is the **Liseberg Pleasure Park**, which includes theatres and restaurants among its many attractions. These are all places that are included in the bus sightseeing tour of the city.

On the opposite side of the Götaälv is the industrial district of Hisingen, which can be reached from the city centre through a tunnel or via one of two long bridges. It includes the Ramberg viewing point, with its wonderful panorama of the city.

There are also several boat excursions available, including a trip to the island fortress of **Nya Älvsborg**, where many battles were fought against the Danes. Some trips include a meal at the fortress. All the boats go from the main harbour piers along Skeppsbron, and bookings can be made at the tourist information office on Kungsportsplatsen.

Museums in Göteborg

Museum of Art (Götaplatsen): works of old masters; French and Scandinavian art; exhibitions in adjoining art gallery.
House of the East India Company (Norra Hamngatan): historical, archaeological and ethnographical collections.
Industrial Museum (Åvägen): the development of industry over three centuries.
Kronhuset (Kronhusgatan): the history of Göteborg.
Military Museum (Skansen Kronan).
Natural History Museum (Slottskogen): mammals, birds, etc.
Rhösska Museum of Applied Art (Vasagatan): furniture, textiles and glass.
Shipping Museum (Stigbergstorget): the history of seafaring, shipbuilding and fisheries.
Museum of Theatrical History (Berzeligatan): the history of theatre in Göteborg.
School Museum (Engelbrektsgatan).
Ship Museum (Lilla Bommen).
Museum of Medical History (Sociale huset).

4 THE GREEN HEART OF SWEDEN

Dalarna and the Great Lakes, Passing Through Some of the Most Beautiful Old Towns

Helsingborg • Jönköping • Ödeshög • Vadstena • Norrköping • Katrineholm • Stockholm • Uppsala • Gävle • Falun • Rättvik • Lake Siljan • Mora • Särna • Malung • Karlstad • Kristinehamn • Mariestad • Lidköping • Vänersborg • Uddevalla • Göteborg

What the Route Has to Offer

This is an ideal route for travellers who do not have enough time to see the whole of Scandinavia, since it offers a taste of everything that there is to be seen in this beautiful part of the world. This is especially true if the detour via Oslo is incorporated. Visitors who come via Denmark will be able to compare it with Sweden.

The route leaves Helsingborg through the rocky landscape of Skåne, and runs past Sweden's two vast inland lakes, Vättern and Vänern. It passes through Södermanland and Uppland — the country of the Svear and cradle of Swedish history, including the ancient cities of Uppsala and Sigtuna, and the islands and skerries off Stockholm. The route moves on, past the old mine workings of Falun, into the endless forests of the north, with their rivers and lakes. This is Dalarna — the true heart of Sweden. It was from Dalarna that Gustav Vasa led his army of peasants to unite the Swedes and liberate them from Danish oppression.

The route continues through the vast forests of Värmland, past lonely lake shores and woods full of elk and capercaillie. In Dalsland there are opportunities to watch how the trees are felled and then made into rafts that are carried along rivers and canals to factories where they are processed into furniture, paper, cellulose or chipboard. The area around Trollhättan and Göteborg is a hive of modern industry, where water power is harnessed towards the creation of steel and finished products such as cars, locomotives and ball-bearings.

This tour can be combined with holidays in either Norway or

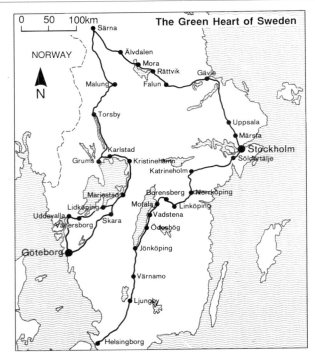

Denmark. Although Helsingborg has been chosen as the starting point, it is equally possible to begin at Göteborg and work the route in reverse. The route can also be made into a circular one by incorporating the section of route 2 that runs along the Kattegat coast between Göteborg and Helsingborg (see page 94).

Transport Connections
There are several ways of travelling to Sweden. The direct sea route from Britain is from Newcastle or Felixstowe to Göteborg (25 and 26½ hours). Some travellers may prefer to travel to Dutch, German or Danish ports, continuing overland and taking a ferry from Denmark to Sweden. The shortest crossing from Denmark to Sweden is the ferry from Helsingør to Helsingborg (25 minutes). There are air services to Stockholm and Göteborg. (For more details see page 168 onwards.)

This tour may be adapted as part of a Norwegian holiday (see *The Visitor's Guide to Norway*). Sections of the tour may also be combined with parts of the other Swedish tours, or may be incorporated as part of a journey to Finland (see *The Visitor's Guide to Finland*).

Length and Timing
The overall length of the route is about 1,700km. Taking into account the amount of time required to get to Sweden, one should probably allow at least a fortnight's travelling time. Those wishing to travel overland via Germany and Denmark should allow longer. Depending on the frequency and length of any stops en route, one could easily require 3 weeks or more altogether.

The Best Time to Travel
The birch trees turn green in the middle of May in southern and central Sweden, but the nights are often still very cold. If the journey is delayed until the second half of June, then even the lakes in Dalarna will be warm enough to bathe in. This is also the midsummer period, when the daytime is long and the nights are barely dark. The best time for bathing is July or August, though the last week in August is often autumnal in areas north of Stockholm.

The Route
Helsingborg (population 100,000) lies at the narrowest point of the Sound (Öresund), opposite the Danish port of Helsingør. At the time when it belonged to Denmark, Helsingborg was an important garrison town. The Sound was fiercely guarded from both sides, and a toll was demanded from every ship that passed into or out of the Baltic. When Skåne was handed over to Sweden, Helsingborg dwindled in importance, and the port did not grow again until relatively recently. The town is dominated by a massive tenth-century tower called the Kärnan. It is 35m high and 60m in diameter, with walls more than 4m thick. From the battlements there is a marvellous view over the town and across the Sound to Helsingør (more familiar in English as Hamlet's Elsinore) and the green roofs of Kronenborg Castle.

Helsing-
borg

It is impossible to miss the E4 motorway from Helsingborg. It is signposted from the harbour for Markaryd and Jönköping. The road first goes left, then sharp right, and then climbs gently through the town. 10km out of Helsingborg there is a turning for the E6, but the E4 carries straight on through the western part of Skåne, which is Sweden's most populous province. The park-like

Helsingborg

landscape is often reminiscent of Denmark or the northernmost parts of Germany. But the wooden houses and farms with their rust-brown paint are quite distinctively Swedish. Skåne also contains Sweden's only coal-mining area, though the coal is somewhat lacking, both in quality and quantity.

The E4 bypasses a number of villages, such as Åstorp, where the R21 goes off towards Kristianstad. In fact the E4 bypasses nearly every town or village on this route. The land begins to rise and the scenery becomes more wooded. The road has risen to 100m by the time it reaches the small country resort of **Örkelljunga** (population 9,000). Just past Örkelljunga, the road passes a lake called Hjälmsjön on the right.

50km
Örkell-
junga

The landscape changes quite markedly. Rocky knolls, worn smooth by glaciers, are interspersed with stretches of forest and farmland. Just before **Markaryd** (population 11,000; altitude 112m), the road crosses into the province of Småland. The word *små* simply means 'small', but in Småland it carries implications of bareness as well. For Småland forms a marked contrast to the

31km
Mark-
aryd

lush, green pastures of Skåne. The road passes Lokasjön and Jetesjön on the left — two of the thousands of lakes with which Småland is peppered. The E4 meets the course of the River Lagan, which it now follows most of the way back to its source.

The road enters more forests, and soon arrives at **Ljungby** (population 26,000; altitude 137m) — a prosperous little town with a variety of wood-processing industries. This area has been settled since prehistoric times, as is shown by the vast number of ancient remains that have been found, such as the Iron Age burial chamber at Kungshögen.

53km
Ljungby

Soon after the village of Lagan, the road meets the shores of Vidöstern — a long, winding lake, enclosed by dense forests, which the road follows for most of its length. At the northern end of the lake is the small town of **Värnamo** (population 14,000; altitude 169m). On a side road from Värnamo to Gnosjö is High Chaparral — a mock-up of the American Wild West, with authentically dressed cowboys in the saloons, and even an iron horse.

44km
Värnamo

The E4 continues through the forests along the course of the Lagan. A short way further on, near the village of Torp, there is an ancient runestone by the side of the road. The scenery opens out on the left into a vast peat bog called Stora Mossen — a typical Småland landscape. The area is thinly populated, with only a sprinkling of villages such as Skillingaryd and Vaggeryd (*ryd* = swamp). About 20km after Vaggeryd, there is a left turn along a small road via Norrahammar to Taberg (altitude 350m) — a bare dome of magnetite, which affords a magnificent view of the area.

The E4 soon arrives at **Jönköping** (population 110,000; altitude 90m). This old industrial town is beautifully situated at the southern end of Lake Vättern. It is the home of the Swedish match industry, the history of which is explained at the Match Museum. The E4 runs along the shore to the industrial town of **Huskvarna** (population 14,000), which has long since been absorbed into the Jönköping conurbation.

75km
Jön-
köping

The E4 turns northward again along the shore of **Lake Vättern**, which is the second-largest of Sweden's 100,000 lakes. It is 130km long, with a width of between 25km and 30km; it has an area of 1,900sq km, and reaches a maximum depth of 125m. The road leaves the shore briefly to cross a hill, and returns to the lakeside by the famous Gyllene Uttern (Golden Otter) Hotel, with its beautiful view of the lake and of the island of **Visingsö**. There is a statue of a runner to the left of the road. It

Brahe Church, Visingsö

75km
Gränna

26km
Ödes-
hög

32km
Vadstena

is of no special interest, since Sweden is full of such statues. At **Gränna** there is an opportunity for a boat trip to Visingsö. This lovely green island has several ruined castles and interesting old churches.

The road keeps to the shore as it crosses into the province of Östergötland. At **Ödeshög** the road forks. The E4 turns inland, while the present route follows the R50 along the shore to **Alvastra**, where there is a ruined twelfth-century Cistercian monastery. The R50 goes on from here through flat, wooded countryside.

It returns to the shore at the old historic town of **Vadstena** (population 5,000). Vadstena was founded in the thirteenth century, when St Birgitta built a convent here, thus founding a new order of nuns. The nunnery was dissolved in 1595, but the building has been preserved in its original state. The old monastic church, known as the Blue Church (Blåkyrkan), has a shrine to St Birgitta. It contains a triptych created by a master from Lübeck in 1549. Down by the harbour is Vadstena Castle, which was built by Gustav Vasa in the Renaissance style. The beautiful chapel is

Church at
Gränna

part of a later extension. The castle was neglected for a long time, ✿
but was restored in the nineteenth century. Vadstena also has
the oldest town hall in Sweden. It was built in the fifteenth
century, and stands next to the market place.

15km
Motala

Further along the shore is **Motala** (population 49,000). The
town is sited at the beginning of the eastern section of the **Göta
Canal**, which links the Kattegat with the Baltic (see page 161).
The western section goes back more than 180 years, while this
eastern section is only 150 years old. The market square at
Motala contains a statue of Count von Platen, who built the canal.
Though an industrial town, Motala is nicely laid out with parks, and
still preserves a pleasant air of cleanliness.

The route leaves Lake Vättern, and goes east along the R36,
which runs along the north shore of Lake Boren as far as
Borensberg. It then follows the southern bank of the Göta Canal
as far as **Vreta Abbey** — a twelfth-century church, which at one ✿
time belonged to a Cistercian convent. To the left of the road is
the massive lock complex of Berg, where the Göta Canal makes

St Birgitta Convent, Vadstena

its biggest drop between Lake Vättern (altitude 88m) and Lake Roxen (altitude 33m).

50km
Lin-
köping

The R36 carries on to **Linköping** (population 110,000; altitude 40m). Linköping is the capital of the province of Östergötland, and was founded in the eleventh century. By the twelfth century it had become one of the most important towns in Sweden. Not much is left of the old parts of the town; most of the old wooden buildings which survived the wars with Denmark were destroyed in the many fires which ravaged the city in subsequent centuries. Gamla (Old) Linköping is an open-air museum to the west of the city (next to the E4); it contains about fifty restored buildings from the eighteenth and nineteenth centuries, most of which are lived in. The cathedral retains a little of its original structure, including the Romanesque north doorway. But most of it was built in the fifteenth century, while the tower was added in 1886. The late Gothic choir was the creation of Master Gerlach of Cologne. In front of the cathedral is a statue of Folke Filbyter, the

Statue of Filbyter, Linköping

legendary ancestor of the Folkung dynasty. It was sculpted by Carl Milles in 1927. The sixteenth-century castle is now the local governor's residence.

The route rejoins the E4, which continues north-eastwards

Kolmården Safari Park

44km
Norr-
köping

from Linköping through a heavily populated region. The road crosses the Göta Canal near Norsholm. 8km further on is Lövstad Castle, which was built in the seventeenth century. From here it is only a short distance to **Norrköping** (population 120,000).

There have been settlements in the Norrköping area since prehistoric times, as is shown by the many Bronze Age rock drawings that have been preserved in Himmelstalund Park — an extensive leisure park to the west of the railway station. The town was first built by King Albert of Mecklenburg in 1384. But it did not become important until the Dutch industrialist De Geer built a textile factory in the town. It has been an important industrial centre ever since, and its favourable position by the shore of Bråviken (a Baltic inlet) has made it into one of Sweden's largest ports.

The modern town is characterised by broad avenues and parks. Of particular interest are the Museum of Art, the Museum of Local History and the cactus gardens, which contain up to 25,000 cacti. Not far away are the remains of the Johannisborg fortifications, which were built in 1613. 6km north-west of the town towards Svärtinge is the Ringstad estate, which includes the remains of a seventh-century Viking fortification and an extensive burial site.

There is a choice of routes from Norrköping to Stockholm. The shorter route via Nyköping is described in route 2 (see page 83). The present route goes further inland via Katrineholm and Mariefred. The two routes meet again at Södertälje (see below).

The route leaves Norrköping on the E4, but at Åby it turns due north along the R56. (To the right is **Kolmården Safari Park**, which is the largest of its kind in Europe.) This road runs through a typical Södermanland landscape, in which the lakes often cover a larger area than the dry land. The next town is **Katrineholm** (population 32,000). 3km south-west of the town is the site of the oldest prehistoric settlement to have been discovered in Sweden. It consists of Stone Age dwellings that are about 5,000 years old.

47km
Katrine-
holm

⌘

The route goes east from Katrineholm along the R57 through a landscape of forests and lakes. Just before Björnlunda, there is a left turn along the L223, which goes on past more forests and lakes. 2km beyond the junction with the E3 is the little town of **Mariefred** (population 2,500). Mariefred is gorgeously situated on the shore of Lake Mälaren, and owes its name to the former Carthusian monastery of Pax Mariae (Peace of St Mary). The author and journalist Kurt Tucholsky, who died in 1936, is buried in the cemetery here. In a park near the railway bridge are several runestones from the Viking period — marvellous examples of earlier Swedish cultures. The town also has a railway museum.

90km
Marie-
fred

⌘

The most important attraction at Mariefred is **Gripsholm Castle**, which stands on an island by the shore, not far from the pier where crowds of weekend visitors arrive on boat trips from Stockholm. Gripsholm is probably the finest and most interesting Renaissance castle in Sweden. The original building was that of Bo Jonsson Grip, who in the fourteenth century was the most powerful landowner in Sweden. Gustav Vasa commissioned the building of the present four-towered structure over the ruins of the old castle. It was finished in 1537, and is a masterpiece of Renaissance architecture. The interior is a real art lovers' paradise. Some of the rooms have their original furniture and décor, while others contain examples from later periods. The theatre, which was added later, is equally interesting. The portrait collection is possibly the largest in the world, with nearly 3,000 pictures.

⌘

The route returns as far as the E3, which it then follows in an easterly direction to **Södertälje** (see page 83). It then joins

29km
Söder-
tälje

Uppsala

35km
Stock-
holm

route 2 for the motorway section from Södertälje to Stockholm. For full details about **Stockholm**, see page 37.

    The E4 motorway leaves Stockholm in a northerly direction. Just past the village of Norrviken, it passes the lovely twelfth-century church of Sollentuna on the left. At Märsta there is a left turn onto the L263, which leads to Sigtuna.

35km
Sigtuna

    Sigtuna (population 4,000) is one of the oldest towns in Sweden. In the eleventh century it was the capital of Sweden and an important centre for trade. In 1187 it was destroyed by invaders from Estonia. It is not known how big the old city was, but the ruins of the tenth- and eleventh-century churches of St Olof, St Per and St Lars bear witness to the extent of its former glory. The lovely eighteenth-century building in the market place is the smallest town hall in Sweden. The main street is also very picturesque. St Mary's Church is pure Gothic in style. It was built in the thirteenth century next to the ruins of St Olof's. Also worth seeing is the fine Gothic chapel in the cemetery opposite the church.

    One place worth visiting if time allows is **Skokloster Castle**, which can be reached from Sigtuna via Erikssund and

Häggeby, or otherwise by boat. Also in the same area are the manor houses of Rosersberg, Steninge and Venngarn, parts of which are open to the public. The route continues northwards from Sigtuna via Haga, Vassuda and Sunnersta, passing through a nature reserve along the shores of Lake Ekoln.

The road soon arrives at **Uppsala** (population 130,000), which is the home of Sweden's oldest university. The ancient city of Uppsala is without doubt one of the most fascinating cities in Europe. In prehistoric times it was the centre of a religious cult. The Swedes were later converted to Christianity, and in 1164 the archbishopric was moved to Uppsala. The city has remained the religious centre of Sweden. The university was founded in 1477. Queen Christine lived in Uppsala for some time during the seventeenth century, and was here when she abdicated. In the great fire of 1702, most of the old city was destroyed. It was quickly rebuilt, and most of the buildings in the old city go back to this period. The only buildings from before the great fire are in the area immediately below the castle. In a wooden tower next to the castle is Uppsala's famous Gunilla Bell, which rings in the new day at six o'clock each morning, and rings out the old one at nine

32km
Uppsala

Old Uppsala

in the evening.

✤ Uppsala Cathedral is the one of the largest in Scandinavia. It is Gothic in style, and was begun in the twelfth century. The spires were destroyed by fire, but were later rebuilt to a height of 118m. In Odinslund, not far from the castle, is Trinity Church, also known as the Peasants' Church. The oldest parts of the building go back to the twelfth century, and are decorated inside with some beautiful medieval wall paintings.

✤ The University Library contains more than two million books and 28,000 manuscripts. Its most valuable possession is Bishop Wulfila's *Silver Bible* — an ancient Gothic version of the four Gospels, written in silver letters on purple parchment. The oldest part of the university is the Gustavianum — a domed building, which was once used for anatomical demonstrations. Linnaeus, the great botanist and taxonomist, worked and taught at Uppsala University. His botanic garden has been restored to its original form, and this, together with the rooms where he worked, has been turned into a museum.

5km to the north of the city is Gamla Uppsala (Old Uppsala), which in pre-Christian times was the capital of the Svear — the tribe from whom the Swedes originated. The old medieval cathedral was built here on the site of the former temple to the god of light. There is now a little stone church on the site, which is built

✤ of remnants of the cathedral. The church is surrounded by burial mounds. They are known as Kungshögarna (the Royal Hills), and go back to the fifth and sixth centuries.

The E4 continues northwards from Uppsala along a very straight stretch of road. It passes through a region steeped in history, with many lovely old churches and other buildings in the villages on the way. There are sites that go back to earliest history, one example being the churchyard at **Vendel,** which is 10km east of the E4 (via a right turn at Läby). 30km east of the main road is the iron-mining area of **Dannemora**, which has

✤ produced high-quality ores since the fifteenth century. The road
59km passes the ancient abbey of Husborgsby. A little further on, there
Tierp is a turning for **Tierp**, which has a fascinating fourteenth-century church.

At Mehedeby the route turns right off the E4, and goes along a small road through Marma. It comes into the R76 near Skutsär on the Gulf of Bothnia. Skutsär lies at the mouth of the Dalälv, and is the collecting point for the wood which is brought down-river from the forests of the interior. The logs wait here to be loaded onto ships. The R76 goes on to **Furuvik**, which has one of the largest amusement parks in Sweden. The next village is **Järvsta**, where a vast number of prehistoric discoveries have been made, including a stone circle in the shape of a ship.

The R76 quickly arrives at **Gävle** (population 85,000), which is the capital of the province of Gästrikland. It is also the main port for the shipping of wood products and ores from the neighbouring mining regions. Nothing is left of its old wooden buildings apart from the carefully restored houses in the open-air museum of Gamle (Old) Gävle. The ancient royal castle was replaced by a palace in the seventeenth century, which now houses the local government headquarters. Visitors will be surprised to discover that Gävle is the site of the most northerly coffee-roasting firm in Europe. Of particular interest is the Museum Silvanum (Forestry Museum).

55km
Gävle

The route now turns westward along the R80, which is initially of motorway standard. It follows the Gävleå (å = river) and the north shore of Storsjön ('the great lake'). The road passes near to the industrial town of **Sandviken** (population 22,000), which has the oldest and largest Bessemer steelworks in the country. The R80 continues through a landscape of continuous forests with lakes. At Edsken it leaves Gästrikland for the province of Dalarna — the so-called green heart of Sweden. The landscape becomes much hillier, while the trees become much taller either side of the road. On the approach to Korsnäs there is a magnificent view of Lake Runn.

25km
Sand-
viken

At the northern end of Lake Runn is the old mining town of **Falun** (population 48,000; altitude 115m). The local mining corporation, the Stora Kopparbergs Bergslag, can be traced back to 1288, and is probably the oldest mining concern in the world. Copper mining is no longer profitable, but there are still plentiful supplies of lead and zinc ores, and also of pyrites. They are processed on the spot into various chemicals. The old copper workings are to the south-west of the town. Parts of them are open to the public, and can be reached via the R80 (Tunavägen). Also of interest are the trenches formed where underground tunnels collapsed, some of which appeared centuries ago. The Stora Kopparbergs Museum contains many exhibits of great interest to the lay person, such as a collection of copper coins, including some weighing more than 20kg. In medieval times these copper mines were Sweden's greatest source of income.

60km
Falun

The route continues along the R80 for Rättvik and Mora. The

*Stora copper
mine, Falun*

road has hardly left Falun before it meets another lake. Lake Varpan is overlooked by **Heden Castle**. The road enters a delightful region of dense, uninhabited forests, which are uninterrupted except by lakes or the odd clearing. After several miles of this beautiful scenery, the road enters the R70 near Söderås, where there is a magnificent panorama of **Lake Siljan**. The best view is from the nearby Vidablik lookout tower. Lake Siljan is the largest and most beautiful lake in Dalarna.

46km
Rättvik

The road drops down to the pretty little town of **Rättvik** (population 4,500; altitude 161m) on the shore of the lake. Rättvik is both a winter and a summer resort. It is famous in winter for its slalom course, which is accessible by ski-lift. In the summer, its gorgeous setting and marvellous facilities make it an ideal centre for a holiday in Dalarna. On a promontory to the north of the town is an old church which goes back to about 1200. In the churchyard is the Vasa Stone — a memorial stone to Gustav Vasa, who led his army from here in 1520 to liberate Sweden from the Danes. Rättvik offers a wide choice of excursions into the surrounding area, whether on foot, by car or by boat.

Tour of Lake Siljan
(140km round trip)

Lake Siljan (area 354sq km) is often known in Swedish as Dalarnas Öga — the Eye of Dalarna. It is surrounded by magnificent scenery, and has thus become popular with holidaymakers. But it is more than that for the Swedes, who give the lake an almost religious significance as the place from which Gustav Vasa led his army to unite the Swedes and liberate them from Denmark. There are plenty of good camping sites along the shores of the lake.

The route leaves Rättvik along the R70 for Mora, which keeps to the shore as far as Vikarbyn. A short way beyond the village there is a right turn leading to a lookout tower on a hill called Röjeråsen (329m), which affords a magnificent view of the lake. The main road moves slightly away from the shore, and continues via Garsås and Färnäs to **Mora** (see below). The road crosses the canal that runs between Lake Siljan and the nearby Orsasjön; from the bridge, there is often an opportunity to watch the timber from the forests being floated along the canal.

The route turns left along the L242, which follows the shore. 10km further on, it turns left again along an unclassified road via Ryssa to **Gesunda**, which lies on the shore at the foot of Gesundabjerget (altitude 501m). A small road leads across from here to the little island of Sollerön, which since time immemorial has been famous for its boat-building. There is also an extensive Viking burial site on the island, on the road between the villages of Sollerön and Bengtsarvet.

The road continues from Gesunda along the wooded shore of the lake. After a bridge over the Limå, the road crosses a spit of land before returning to the shore just past Alvik-Grytnäs. At this point the lake forms a fjord-like inlet called Osterviken.

At the southern tip of the inlet is the small town of **Leksand** (population 4,000). Leksand is famous for its sawmills, and is a popular holiday resort, especially in midsummer. It has a twelfth-century church, which is built out on a promontory on the site of a pre-Christian temple. This church has long been famous as a centre for midsummer celebrations. The first Sunday in July is the traditional day for the festival of the church boats. These boats were originally used to bring worshippers from the surrounding area, and are shaped like the ancient Viking ships. At the same time of year, the local people stage an open-air performance of the Himlaspel — a traditional mystery play based on a local

Belfry at Leksand Church

legend.

The route continues along the shore of the lake to the small village of Tällberg, which lies immediately below Plintsberg (altitude 365m) — another hill with a lookout tower. From here it is only a short distance back to **Rättvik**.

Rättvik 38km Mora

The main route continues from **Rättvik** along the R70, which runs north-west along the shore of Lake Siljan to **Mora** (population 17,000). This modern bathing resort is clustered round a lovely old village, which retains numerous mementoes of the Vasa period. Mora is on the canal running between Lake Siljan and the nearby Orsasjön, and there is often an opportunity to watch the timber from the forests as it floats past along the canal.

The old fourteenth-century church has a separate bell tower. In front of it is a statue of Gustav Vasa — a work by the famous painter and sculptor Andreas Zorn, who lived and worked in Mora and is buried in the churchyard. Zorngården, the house where he lived, is now open to the public, while the Zorn Museum contains a collection of his works. There is also the artist's former studio, and Zorns Gammelgård — an open-air museum made up of old wooden houses, which Zorn himself collected from all over

Dalarna. The oldest of these buildings is over 600 years old.

Not far away is the cellar where Gustav Vasa is said to have hidden during his flight from the Danes. The house above it is full of mementoes of Gustav Vasa. The Gustav Vasa story is described on page 123, together with the famous Vasa Run — a cross-country skiing race which commemorates the story. The race starts at Sälen and finishes here at Mora.

Short Cut from Mora to Malung (73km)

If time is severely limited, it is possible to take a short cut by travelling direct from Mora to Malung. This route goes along the L242, which runs through forests and hills past the Siljanfors Forest Museum, which also has a café and an interesting nature trail. At Johannisholm, the route turns right along the L234, which continues through endless forests, past the lakeside resort of Öje, to **Malung** (see page 124).

The longer route through Nörredalarna is thoroughly to be recommended, since it crosses into the vast eternal forests of northern Sweden — forests which are still inhabited by bears, and where elk and reindeer may be seen browsing by the roadside. There are side-roads into the mountains that go right up to the Norwegian border, and into areas where skiing is possible up to the end of June. This is a marvellously hospitable region, in which excellent hotel, chalet and camping accommodation can be found in close proximity to wild, unspoilt forests.

The route goes north-west from **Mora** along the L295, which Mora follows the course of the Österdalälv through a mostly unin- 40km habited region to **Älvdalen** (population 8,400; altitude 238m). Älvdalen Älvdalen, with its fifteenth-century church, forms the main cultural and economic centre of southern Nörredalarna. It is a region noted for its arts and crafts, which are pursued during the long winter months. Some of the most popular items available are carvings and handwoven goods.

The tourist office next to the station is open throughout the year, and provides information in English about the local tourist facilities. There is a wide choice of accommodation available, from hotel rooms or holiday flats to an excellent camping site by a heated swimming pool. The area is a paradise for anglers. The waters to the south of Älvdalen are particularly rich in valuable species of fish, such as the salmon trout, which can weigh up to

Zorngården, Mora

4kg, and the red trout, noted for its marvellous flavour. Fishing licences for the various rivers and lakes can be obtained from the tourist office.

The region is interesting geologically on account of its porphyry deposits. This ancient red rock has been quarried here since the seventeenth century. The original old quarry (Gamla Porfyrverket) was founded by King Carl XVI Johan as a means of relieving local poverty. Carl Johan's sarcophagus was made here. It took 8 years to make; it was carried down the frozen river on a sledge to the port of Gävle, and then taken on by ship to the royal mausoleum on the Stockholm island of Riddarholmen. The old quarry was closed down in 1890, but the quarry inspector's lovely old wooden house has been preserved as an annexe to the Älvdalen Hotel. A new quarry was begun to the west of Älvdalen, where porphyry is still processed in the same traditional way to produce a wide variety of decorations and ornaments. The quarry and its associated works are very well worth a visit.

The summit of **Väsagnupen** (altitude 482m) can be reached by cable car from the nearby village of Väsa. There is a well-

appointed mountain inn by the cable-car terminus. The view from
the top is magnificent, and extends right across to Lake Siljan. It
also provides a clear impression of the local settlement pattern.
For Älvdalen is not a single self-contained unit, but an amorphous
settlement round a church, which serves as the centre for the
numerous hamlets and buildings that are scattered within a radius
of about 12km.

One of these settlements is the lovely old Rotskans Estate,
which is built around the ruins of a tower that was erected during
the Danish wars in the seventeenth century. The estate has been
opened to the public as a kind of open-air museum. Two of the
chapels from the old, scattered parish have been re-erected on
the site. Of these, the sixteenth-century chapel from Evertsberg
has a fifteenth-century altar shrine, which originally came from
Lübeck in Germany, while the eighteenth-century chapel from
Åsen contains a seventeenth-century altarpiece from the
Evertsberg Chapel. Such chapels were mostly used as schools,
and had services only three times a year.

North of Älvdalen is the Navadalen Nature Reserve, which
includes a small tourist village. This is an area still inhabited by
bears, which is also interesting for its traditional pastoral
economy. There are still between thirty and forty Alpine-type
dairies, producing milk products according to traditional methods.

The route continues north-west from **Älvdalen** along the Älvdalen
L295. After Åsen, the road leaves the Österdaläv for a short
distance. The scenery becomes wilder as the road climbs through
dense, mostly uninhabited forests, while the mountains either
side become higher. The road runs along the side of the long,
winding Trängletsjön. At one time this lake was a gorge, through
which the Österdaläv ran in a magnificent series of rapids. But in
1960 the valley was blocked by a 120m high dam (the biggest in
Sweden) as part of a massive hydroelectric scheme.   81km

The road arrives at **Särna** (population 1,200; altitude 444m) —   Särna
the most northerly point of the route. Särna is beautifully situated
by Trängletsjön. It has a lovely old wooden church, which,
though originally built in 1244, was heavily restored in the
eighteenth century. Those wishing to travel on into northern
Sweden should join route 5 from Särna onwards (see page 141).

Excursion to Idre and Beyond
This short excursion goes further up into the mountains on the

*Views in Sweden
are magnificent*

L295, continuing along the course of the Österdalälv. At Älvros the L311 goes off to the left (see route 5, page 141). 32km from Särna is the mountain resort of **Idre**, which is in an area full of mountain inns and tourist villages. A newly-built mountain road leads on further up to Idre Hotellet on the slopes of Längfjället, close to the Norwegian border, where the skiing season lasts well into the summer.

Särna The route turns sharply southward from **Särna** along the L297. After a short distance there is a turning along a small mountain road to **Mickeltemplet** — a viewing point with a restaurant. It commands a magnificent view of Fulufjället — the nearby mountain range that straddles the Norwegian border.

The L297 continues southward through a largely uninhabited region of continuous forest, interrupted only by lakes. It frequently passes a shelter by the roadside — a small hut with a fireplace and a supply of firewood. This is the area where the reindeer come furthest south; the herds here belong to five resident families of Lapps. Near **Fulunäs** a road goes off to the right towards the Norwegian border. It crosses the frontier after

Vasa Ski Run

17km, and eventually leads to Road 3 from Kongsvinger to Trondheim (see *The Visitor's Guide to Norway*).

The present route continues southward along the valley of the Västerdalälv to the small village of **Sälen**. High up on the mountainside above Sälen is a large tourist hotel (altitude 800m), which can be reached from the village by a good, well-surfaced road. It has a heated swimming pool and good skiing facilities which can be used well into the summer months.

72km
Sälen

Sälen is the starting point for the famous Vasa Run — a cross-country skiing race across the mountains to Mora (see page 118). It commemorates Gustav Vasa, who in 1521 formed a peasant army in Dalarna and led a decisive campaign against the Danish rulers. The Swedes eventually won, and in 1523 Gustav was crowned King of Sweden, thus founding the Vasa dynasty.

The race is based on the story of Gustav Vasa himself. In 1521, following the failure of his first campaign against the Danes, Gustav Vasa was being hunted by the Danish army. He hid in a cellar in Mora (which still exists and is open to the public), and then tried to escape by skiing towards the Norwegian border. But the peasants thought otherwise, and sent two of their best skiers after him. They caught up with him at Sälen, and persuaded him to return. Thus began his final successful campaign against the Danes.

The Vasa Run takes place annually in March. The competitors ski across country over a distance of 85km from Sälen to Mora. The race is extremely popular in Sweden, with more than 8,000 active participants of all ages from all over Sweden and elsewhere.

65km
Malung
The route continues southwards, following the course of the Västerdalälv, until it reaches **Malung** (population 12,000; altitude 302m). Malung is an important centre for the leather industry.

The route turns south-east along the L234. The wild upland scenery is made up of vast forests and peat bogs. (Travellers are advised not to stray from the road.) This is elk country, as can be seen from the tracks which they leave all over the place. At Granberget, in the centre of the peat moors, the road crosses from Dalarna into the province of Värmland. At Värnäs it comes down into the valley of the Klarälv — a river which comes down from the fjells (high plateaux) of Norway, and which runs all the way through Värmland until it enters Lake Vänern at Karlstad.

The L234 follows the broad valley for only a short distance. It then crosses the Klarälv near Nörre Ny, and after Osebol climbs back into the upland forests and boglands, past occasional rocky outcrops. The road turns south again, and descends through a landscape of forests, lakes and rivers to the small town of

95km
Torsby
Torsby, which is prettily situated at the northern end of Lake Övre Fryken (Upper Fryken).

Cross-route into Norway via Kongsvinger and Oslo

Torsby
This route goes from **Torsby** along a small unclassified road to Rådom. The road is unmetalled, but is nonetheless not too uneven. It runs along a river bank through dense forests, which are occasionally interrupted by pastures. It passes between two beautiful little lakes called Flaten and Veden, and goes through

22km
Östmark
the villages of Sörmark and **Östmark**. Both were founded by Finnish settlers in the sixteenth and seventeenth centuries. Östmark has an eighteenth-century wooden church, which is Finnish in style.

The road climbs through hills covered in forests, and keeps crossing a fast mountain stream called the Röjdå. There are some nice places to camp on the river bank near the bridges. After

Röjdåfors the road comes to a lake which straddles the national 20km
Norwegian
border frontier. It is called Stora Röjdan in Swedish and Stora Røgden in Norwegian. The customs post is by the shore of the lake.

The road enters Road 205, which descends through dense forests, passing through Lunderseter on the way to Kongsvinger. 35km
Roverud At **Roverud** the road enters Road 3, which follows the course of the Glomma. The Glomma is the longest river in Scandinavia, and carries the largest volume of water of any river in Norway, making it important for the production of hydroelectricity. The landscape now changes as the forests open up into gently undulating fields.

The road quickly arrives at the old fortified town of 9km
Kongs-
vinger **Kongsvinger** (population 23,000; altitude 135m). The fortress above the town commands a magnificent view of the Glomma valley. The route leaves Kongsvinger along Road 2 for Oslo, which continues along the Glomma valley until it leaves it at Nes. It enters the E6 at **Kløfta**, and from here it is only a short 63km
Kløfta distance to the Norwegian capital.

Full details about **Oslo** and connecting routes through Norway 31km
Oslo are given in *The Visitor's Guide to Norway*. Those wishing to return to Sweden are recommended to follow the route described on page 91.

The main route goes south from **Torsby** on the L234, which runs Torsby along the shore of Lake Övre Fryken (Upper Fryken) to the 42km
Sunne holiday resort of **Sunne**. Sunne is delightfully situated between Lakes Övre Fryken and Mellan Fryken (Middle Fryken). The accommodation and facilities are excellent (hotels, holiday villages, camping sites, a swimming pool, etc).

This part of Värmland was the setting for Selma Lagerlöf's novel *Gösta Berling*, which takes place in several wooded estates by the shores of the three long lakes called Övre, Mellan and Nedre (Lower) Fryken. The author was teaching in Landskrona at the time when she wrote the novel in 1887. But she was born on the family estate of **Mårbacka**, which is 9km to the south-east of Sunne. The family had lost the estate on the death of her father, but thanks to her success as a novelist, she was eventually able to buy it back. She first used the house as a summer residence, but later had it extended, and lived there permanently for the rest of her life. After her death in 1940, the house and estate were preserved as a museum to her memory. They are exactly as they were during her lifetime, and are open to

*Rottneros
Sculpture Park*

the public from 15 May to 15 September. Selma Lagerlöf is buried at the cemetery in Östra Ämtervik, a few kilometres south of Mårbacka.

Immediately to the south of Sunne is Länsmansgården, which was the residence of a former high-court judge. It is now part of a hotel complex, but the rooms are still decorated in the style of nineteenth-century Swedish high society.

The L234 continues southwards along the shore of Lake Mellan Fryken. A few kilometres further on is **Rottneros Manor** — a neo-classical structure, built on the site of the legendary Ekeby Manor, which was burnt down in 1929. The estate includes a marvellous sculpture park, created by the industrialist Svart Påhlsson. The 40 hectare site contains a unique collection of 100 sculptures from the ancient, classical and modern periods. The park is open to the public, and has more than 300,000 visitors every year.

The L234 moves away from the lakeshore. Then there is a left turn into the R61, which meets the southern end of Lake Nedre Fryken near St Kil's Chapel. The R61 turns south again, and soon 71km Karlstad arrives at **Karlstad** (population 72,000), which is beautifully

The area around Vänersborg has a large elk population

situated on an island by the shore of Lake Vänern. The town has been important since the Middle Ages, but most of the old wooden buildings were destroyed by fire in 1865. Karlstad is the capital of the province of Värmland, and the home of several large wood-processing firms.

The route continues on the E18 along the wooded northern shore of Lake Vänern, which can occasionally be glimpsed from between the trees. From Karlstad to Kristinehamn, the route follows route 2 in reverse (see page 89). **Lake Vänern** (altitude 41m) is the largest lake in Sweden, having a total area of 5,546sq km. It was originally formed by faulting in the south Swedish basin, which was still covered by sea at the end of the Ice Age. When the sea later retreated, Lake Vänern and the other Swedish lakes gradually turned to freshwater lakes as they were fed by the rivers. Lake Vänern is a busy trade route, and forms a major section of the Göta Canal waterway that links Stockholm and Göteborg.

At the north-eastern corner of Lake Vänern is the industrial port of **Kristinehamn** (population 28,000), which is important for the trans-shipment of iron and timber from the hinterland via the

45km
Kristine-
hamn

Göta Canal to Göteborg on the Skagerrak and Stockholm on the Baltic.

The route leaves the E18 at Kristinehamn, turning south along the R64, which runs parallel to the eastern shore of Lake Vänern but at some distance from it. At Edet the L204 comes in from the north-east. There is also a turning to the south-east along a side-road to the picturesque little village of Söder Råda, where the church, built in 1350, contains a number of frescos. The R64 now follows the shore of Lake Vänern, leaving it only briefly, until at **Sjötorp** it crosses the **Göta Canal** (see page 161). The canal reaches Lake Vänern from Göteborg; it continues from Sjötorp to Karlsborg on Lake Vättern, which it then leaves at Motala.

80km
Marie-
stad

10km further·on, the road enters the E3, and then soon arrives at **Mariestad** (population 26,000). The town was completely rebuilt following a fire in the nineteenth century. The only old buildings to have survived are the fifteenth-century valley church, with its massive tower, and the castle on an island in the River Tida, which was built in 1660. Now the seat of local government, it also houses a museum.

Detour via Lidköping, Trollhättan and the Coast
This detour is 90km longer than the direct route to Göteborg, but the scenery is much more interesting. It is therefore greatly to be recommended if time is available.

Marie-
stad

50km
Lid-
köping

The route goes from **Mariestad** along the E3, which leaves the shore of Lake Vänern. At Götene it turns right along the L44, which returns to the shore where the lake forms a bay called Kinneviken. Beside Kinneviken is the old town of **Lidköping** (population 35,000) — the home of the Swedish porcelain industry — which has some interesting old buildings. The old hunting lodge by the market square was turned into the town hall in 1670, and is now a museum.

67km
Väners-
borg

The L44 continues via Grästorp to **Vänersborg** (population 34,000), which is on a promontory that sticks out into Lake Vänern. It is protected to the south by a sixteenth-century moat.

The tourist office organises safaris into the area around, which has the largest elk population in the world.

Visitors to Vänersborg are recommended to make a short extra detour to **Trollhättan**, which is 10km to the south along the R45 (see page 94). At one time the Götaälv fell more than 35m within the space of 1.5km over the famous falls at Trollhättan. The river

Habo Church, Västergötland

Ängsö Castle, Västmanland

The island of Frösö

has now been harnessed to produce 200,000kW of electricity, making Trollhättan into the biggest source of energy for industry in southern Sweden.

The route continues along the R44, which goes from 31km Vänersborg to **Uddevalla**. Here it enters the E6, which comes Udde-south from Oslo, forming one of Scandinavia's main north-south valla links. The coastal section which follows can be combined with either of the two detours into Norway which are described in this book (see pages 90 and 124).

The route goes south from Uddevalla along the E6, which soon 20km arrives at **Ljungskile** on the shores of the Håkefjord. On the Ljung-opposite side of the fjord is the island of Orust, which has a large skile number of excellent beaches and camping sites. It can be reached by means of several new road bridges via the island of Tjörn to the south.

The E6 continues via Jörlända and Kareby (with its old church) 71km to the ancient town of **Kungälv** (population 28,000). The first Kungälv record of Kungälv goes back as far as the ninth century, when it was called Kongahalla. Down the centuries, the town has frequently been destroyed by fire. The old Baroque church was built in 1679. The E6 motorway leaves Kungälv to the south via a bridge over the Nordre Älv — a branch of the Götaälv. It passes the ruins of the famous Bohus Castle, which was built by King ⌘ Håkon of Norway in the fourteenth century, and which gave its name to the province of Bohuslän.   20km

The route enters **Göteborg** (population 450,000) through its Göte-industrial northern suburbs. For a detailed description of the city, borg see page 96.

Short Detour via Skövde and Hornborgsjön

Travellers who take the direct route to Göteborg may wish to make a short detour between Mariestad and Skara, which includes items of interest to sport and fitness enthusiasts, and to ornithologists. The route involves no more than an extra 20km.

It goes due south from Mariestad along the R48 to **Skövde**. Skövde Skövde has one of Sweden's most up-to-date sports centres. The centre concentrates specifically on medical aspects of sport, including rehabilitation therapy and fitness courses. The centre has some of the world's most up-to-date equipment.

In the immediate vicinity is a lake which attracts ornithologists from all over the world. Every year in the second half of April, the

Horn-
borgs-
jön marshlands around **Hornborgsjön** are a meeting ground for thousands of cranes during their migration from their winter quarters in the south to their nesting sites in north-eastern Europe. The cranes stop to mate here at Hornborgsjön, and their elaborate courtship rituals can be watched undisturbed from specific viewing points around the area.

The route turns west at Skövde along the R49, and rejoins the main route at **Skara**.

Marie-
stad The direct route along the E3 from **Mariestad** to Göteborg is shorter and much faster, but the scenery is less interesting than that on the longer detour suggested above. The direct route is therefore only to be recommended if time is short before the return ferry departs from Göteborg. The E3 goes directly from
45km
Skara Mariestad to **Skara**.

It continues through a mostly cultivated landscape typical of
127km the western part of Västergötland. The road is a fast one, and the
Göte- last section into **Göteborg** has been turned into a motorway.
borg The route to the ferries is well-signposted from the outskirts of the city.

5 TO THE ARCTIC CIRCLE AND BACK

Through the Forests and Lakes of Northern Sweden

Stockholm • Södertälje • Strängnäs • Enköping • Borlänge •
Rättvik • Mora • Särna • Tännäs • Östersund • Lövberga • Dorotea •
Stensele • Arvidsjaur • Jokkmokk • Luleå • Skellefteå • Umeå •
Örnsköldsvik • Härnösand • Sundsvall • Gävle • Stockholm

What the Route has to Offer

Described simply, this route goes from Stockholm via the interior
of Sweden to the Arctic Circle, then returns to Stockholm along
the coast of the Gulf of Bothnia. It may be used as a tour in its
own right, or else may be combined with other routes. The great
Lapland tour of Finland (see *The Visitor's Guide to Finland*) and
the Arctic tour of Norway (see *The Visitor's Guide to Norway*)
combine particularly well with this route. Suitable connecting
routes are included in the route description.

To a certain extent, this tour builds on both route 2 and route 4.
It begins at the elegant and bustling metropolis of Stockholm (see
page 37), and passes into the province of Dalarna, which is not
only steeped in history, but is full of the most gorgeous scenery,
where lakes and forests combine in glorious harmony. The route
passes imperceptibly from the shores of Lake Siljan to the lonely
fastnesses of Härjedalen and Jämtland, and thence to the wild
uplands of southern Lapland, where the stunted woodlands have
adapted to the frosts and the long nights of winter, and survive
among the rocks and tundra of the north. The route returns along
the east coast of Sweden, past large, busy harbours that are
used mostly for shipping timber. The last part of the route goes
close to islands and skerries where bathing is possible in
summer.

There is so much to see in the north, from the thousands of
lakes and the logs borne along fast-flowing rivers, to the wild
forests and moorlands. The north offers more than just a pair of
reindeer antlers to take home as a souvenir. Indeed, during the

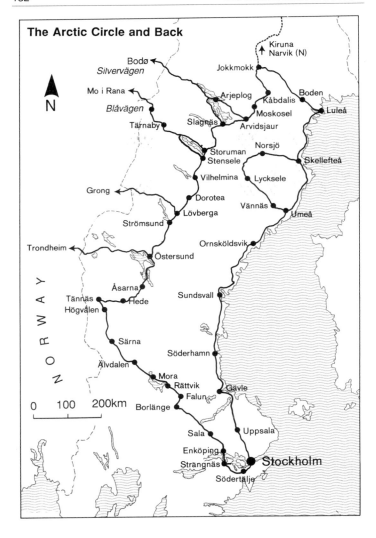

The Lapp Gate, Lapland

summer, one is unlikely to glimpse any of the reindeer in their natural environment. The nomadic Lapps depend on them, but they again are elsewere in the summer, following the herds across their remote summer pastures. The most one is likely to see on this tour are a few of the 'town Lapps' who live from the tourist trade; they will pose for cameras in their picturesque costumes, or sell souvenirs such as reindeer skins and antlers. The leather goods are particularly good, for the *Sameh* (as the Lapps call themselves) are renowned as producers of strong, fine leather.

The tour also crosses into the land of the midnight sun, about which much is said and little is really understood (see page 35). A Swede once commented, 'At midsummer the days are so long and sunny, and after the long nights of winter the warmth, light and life send us wild!' This comment may provide some insight into the Swedish mentality, especially that of the impressionable younger Swedes.

The tour also offers glimpses of Sweden's two main sources of wealth: mining and timber — and of the natural resources that enable the Swedes to make use of the wealth: water power and the hydroelectric power that can be produced from it. For in the absence of coal it is hydroelectricity that enables the Swedes to mine and process the ores economically. And although the rivers often pass over too many rapids and falls to be navigable by boat,

Fishing at Norrbotten, Lapland

they provide a cheap means of transporting wood through wild regions that would be too difficult and expensive to traverse by lorry. The cost of floating a log down-river from the interior to the coast is less than the value of a stamp on a letter.

Sweden possesses some of Europe's best rivers for salmon and trout, often in close proximity to roads. Permission is sometimes needed to fish these waters, but it can usually be obtained easily and cheaply from the police or local authorities.

Finally, there are two items which should not be forgotten: a camera, because there is so much to photograph; and a spare can of petrol, since petrol stations are few and far between in the extreme north.

Transport Connections

The shortest route by car is overland, either via the E3 from Göteborg or via the E4 from Helsingborg. This can be varied by using parts of route 4, whether from Helsingborg via Jönköping to Stockholm (see pages 103-112), or by following it in reverse from Göteborg to join route 4 at Särna (see pages 121-129). Parts of route 2 may be used instead, such as the scenic south-east coastal route from Helsingborg to Stockholm (see pages 62-85) or (in reverse) from Göteborg to Stockholm (see pages 88-94).

This assumes that one arrives from Britain by car ferry, either at Göteborg directly from Newcastle or Felixstowe, or at Helsingborg, having travelled overland from Dutch, German or Danish ports. Visitors from the US or those from Britain with less time to spare may care to fly to Stockholm and hire a car from there. Another possible route is via the Newcastle to Oslo ferry, using one of the cross-routes described on pages 90 and 124.

The return journey can of course follow the reverse of one of the routes suggested above. Visitors who combine this tour with the Arctic tour of Norway may wish to travel via Norwegian ports such as Bergen or Oslo (see *The Visitor's Guide to Norway*). Similarly, those who continue their journey through Finland have the opportunity to return by ferry from there and finish their holiday with a trip through southern Sweden.

Length and Timing

The whole tour is 2,700km long from Stockholm to Jokkmokk and back again. However, if one adds between 500km and 600km each way for overland access through Sweden, the journey altogether will amount to at least 3,700km, or over 4,000km if detours are included. One must also take into account the fact that the roads are less good in the north, and that some are unsurfaced, making the journey a much slower one. All things considered, one is well advised to allow a minimum of $3^1/2$ weeks for the journey, adding extra days for any planned stops on the way.

The Best Time to Travel

The regions near the Arctic Circle often have night frosts up to the end of May, while the sea and lakes will not be warm enough to bathe in until the second half of July. On the other hand, the midnight sun is limited to the period between 14 June and 4 July, so those who wish to experience this should plan their tour so as

Sala Silver Mine

to cross the Arctic Circle during this period. In areas north of Dalarna, the weather becomes noticeably autumnal in the second half of August. The best time to travel, therefore, is between 15 June and 20 August. The first part of this period is better for the midnight sun, while the last part is preferable for bathing.

The Route

Stock-
holm
35km
Söder-
tälje
48km
Sträng-
näs

The route leaves **Stockholm** (see page 37) along the E3/E4 motorway for **Södertälje** (population 78,000 — see page 83). At Södertälje it turns onto the E3. At Marielund there is a turning for Mariefred and Gripsholm Castle (5km there and back — see page 111). The route continues along the E3 to **Strängnäs** (population 8,300 — see page 88). Just before entering the town, it turns right over a bridge onto the L55.

The L55 goes north across Lake Mälaren, which it crosses by means of bridges and causeways. Lake Mälaren is the third-largest lake in Sweden, with an area of 1,140sq km; it is 117km long from west to east. This lake is difficult to think of as a single entity, since it is greatly fragmented by thousands of islands and peninsulas. Indeed, it is almost divided into two at the point where the L55 crosses it. Just north of the lake is the town of **Enköping** (population 31,000 — see page 88), which the present route bypasses.

33km
En-
köping

The route goes north-west from Enköping along the R70 through a flat, wooded landscape. The next town is **Sala** (population 11,000; altitude 53m). Sala was important in the Middle Ages on account of its rich silver deposits. A few of the old mines are open to the public. The mines reach a maximum depth of 300m, and have an overall length of 20km. Sala at one time produced an output of more than 3 tonnes of silver per year, and was therefore known as the treasure chest of the Swedish empire. Production is nowadays limited to a small quantity of zinc and lead.

46km
Sala

The R70 continues north-west in a straight line through a region of extensive, mostly uninhabited forests, passing a number of small lakes on the way. The road eventually arrives at the old copper town of **Avesta** (population 27,500) — the first town in the administrative region of Kopparbergs län, which roughly coincides with the old province of Dalarna (*kopparberg* = copper mine). Avesta was once the town where copper was made from the ores that were mined in Falun (see page 115). It now has steel and aluminium plants instead. The Dalälv falls have been partially harnessed for hydroelectric power, but they are still fairly impressive when the water level is high. Not far away are the Norberg iron ore deposits, which have been worked sinced the Middle Ages. Here also was the estate of Engelbrekt Engel-brektsson, who led the peasants' rebellion in 1433.

38km
Avesta

The landscape becomes hillier as the road climbs gently along the course of the Dalälv, which at one point runs through **Lake Hovran**. The road enters **Hedemora** (population 18,000; altitude 105m) on the western shore of the lake. Hedemora is the oldest town in Dalarna. The R70 continues past forests, heathlands and lakes. 20km further on, a spire becomes visible through the trees. It belongs to the fifteenth-century church of Stora Tuna, which was once the religious centre of the province of Dalarna. The church is one of the most perfect of its period in the north. It has a Gothic exterior, while the interior is Baroque.

20km
Hede-
mora

A short way further on is the modern industrial town of **Borlänge** (population 46,000; altitude 140m). 20km to the north-east of here along the R60 is the old copper-mining town of Falun (see page 115). But the present route continues north-westwards along the R70, which climbs gently through the forest as the hills either side become higher.

44km
Borlänge

The road goes through Insjön and crosses a ridge to the small town of **Leksand** (population 4,000; altitude 161m), which lies at

66km
Leksand

Midsummer celebrations

the southern end of Lake Siljan. Leksand is a popular holiday resort, especially in midsummer. Its twelfth-century church is built out on a promontory, on the site of a pre-Christian temple. The church has long been famous as a centre for midsummer celebrations. The first Sunday in July is the traditional day for the festival of the church boats. These boats were originally used to bring Sunday worshippers from the surrounding area, and are shaped like the ancient Viking ships. At the same time of year, the local people stage an open-air performance of the Himlaspel — a traditional mystery play based on a local legend.

The route continues along the shore of **Lake Siljan** (area 354sq km), which is also known in Sweden as Dalarnas Öga — the Eye of Dalarna. Its pretty little lakeside villages and mag- nificent scenery have made it a popular holiday destination. But Lake Siljan is more than that for the Swedes, for whom it has national significance as the place from which Gustav Vasa led his army of peasants to unite the Swedes and liberate them from Denmark. There are plenty of good camping sites along the shores of the lake. The next village is Tällberg. Immediately above it is Plintsberg (altitude 365m) — a hill with a lookout tower commanding a beautiful view of the lake.

20km
Rätt-
vik

A short way further along the lakeshore is the town of **Rättvik** (population 4,500; altitude 161m). Rättvik is popular in winter for its slalom course, which is accessible by ski-lift. This is of less interest in the summer, but its gorgeous setting and marvellous facilities still make it an ideal centre for a summer holiday. On a promontory to the north-west of the town is an old church which was built in 1200, and which has some lovely frescos inside. It is surrounded by a cluster of little wooden huts, which at one time provided overnight accommodation for worshippers from a distance. In the churchyard is the Vasa Stone — a memorial stone to Gustav Vasa, who led his army from here in 1520 to liberate Sweden from the Danes. Rättvik offers a wide choice of excursions into the surrounding area, whether on foot, by car or by boat.

From Rättvik as far as Särna, the route is exactly the same as route 4 (see pages 118-121). The R70 leaves Rättvik in a north-westerly direction along the shore of Lake Siljan. A short way beyond the village of Vikarbyn, there is a right turn leading to a lookout tower on a hill called Röjeråsen (329m), which affords a magnificent view of the lake.

The main road moves away from the shore, and continues via Garsås and Färnäs to **Mora** (population 17,000). This modern lakeside resort is clustered round a lovely old village, which retains numerous mementoes of the Vasa period. Mora is on the canal which runs between Lake Siljan and the nearby Orsasjön, and there is often an opportunity to watch the logs from the forests floating past along the canal.

38km
Mora

The old fourteenth-century church has a separate bell tower.

Chalets near Funäsdalen

In front of it is a statue of Gustav Vasa, which was created by the famous painter and sculptor Andreas Zorn. Zorn lived and worked in Mora, and is buried in the churchyard. Zorngården, the house where he lived, is open to the public, and the Zorn Museum houses a collection of his works. Then there is the artist's former studio, and Zorns Gammelgård — an open-air museum made up of old wooden houses, which Zorn himself 'collected' from all over Dalarna. The oldest of these buildings is over 600 years old.

Not far away is the cellar where Gustav Vasa is said to have hidden during his flight from the Danes. The house above it is full of mementoes of Gustav Vasa. Mora is at the end of the famous Vasa Run — a cross-country skiing race that takes place every March, and which is based on the story of Gustav Vasa. The course is 85km long, and runs from Sälen to Mora; there are as many as 8,000 competitors altogether. The race is described in more detail on page 122, together with the story which it commemorates.

The R70 ends at Mora, which lies just north of the 61st parallel. The route continues along the L295, which follows the course of the Österdalälv. The road climbs gently through an area of dense forests to **Älvdalen** (population 8,400; altitude 238m). Älvdalen is a popular holiday resort, and has a beautiful fifteenth-century church. The area around Älvdalen is particularly interesting. For more details of this, see page 119.

41km
Älvdalen

The road carries on up the valley. After Åsen it leaves the Österdalälv for a short distance. The scenery becomes wilder as the road climbs through dense, mostly uninhabited forests, while the mountains either side become higher. The road runs along the side of the long, winding Tränsgletsjön. At one time this lake was a gorge, through which the Österdalälv ran in a magnificent series of rapids. But in 1960 the valley was blocked by a 120m high dam (the biggest in Sweden) as part of a massive hydroelectric scheme.

81km
Särna

The road arrives at **Särna** (population 1,200; altitude 444m), which is beautifully situated by the shore of Tränsgletsjön. It has a lovely old wooden church, which was originally built in 1244 and was heavily restored in the eighteenth century. At Särna the L297 comes in from Malung (see page 124).

The route carries on for a short while along the course of the Österdalälv. But after 18km it leaves both the river and the L295, and branches off to the north along the L311, which climbs steeply between two ranges of mountains — Nypfället (1192m) to the west and Häggingpfället to the east. This is another popular skiing area. At Kölåsen the road goes over the River Storfjäten, and crosses into the mountainous province of Härjedalen. The section after **Sörvattnet** is a very hilly one. The road passes through Högvålen (the highest village in Sweden), and crosses the Mjostöten Pass (916m). It then descends past a number of small fishing lakes famous among anglers.

61km
Sörvatt-
net

The next village is **Tännäs** (population 1,000; altitude 670m). Here the L311 turns sharply to the right, and then comes into the L312, which forms a connecting route into Norway. Like most of the cross-routes into Norway from Sweden, it runs up a river valley in a north-westerly direction. It then crosses the border mountains towards Røros and Trondheim (see *The Visitor's Guide to Norway*).

40km
Tännäs

Detour via Ljungdalen
(126km Tännäs to Åsarna)

This detour is a particularly scenic one, but is not shown on the map because the road is so difficult and rough. It is unmade, and is only really passable in dry weather. The route goes from **Tännäs** along the L312 towards the Norwegian border. At Funäsdalen, 16km further on, it turns right off the L312, and then forks right again for Storvallen. The road which now follows is the

Tännäs

highest in Sweden. It rises steeply through wild, uninhabited mountains with some magnificent views. Near Storvallen it drops down into the valley of the Mittaälv, then climbs sharply again to over 1,000m, often passing above the tree line.

48km Ljung-dalen

The road eventually drops down into **Ljungdalen** (population 1,000; altitude 615m). This province of Härjedalen is the only Swedish province without a town in it, the largest place being Sveg with just over 2,000 inhabitants. It is popular for winter sports. It has no camping sites as such, but is ideal camping country. From Ljungdalen there is an 18km walk to the Helagsfjället tourist station (1,033m). From here it is an easy $3^1/2$ hour climb to the summit of Helagsfjället (1,796m), which provides a view of Sweden's most southerly glacier. The whole walk from Ljungdalen can be achieved easily in a day. But even without it, the journey is quite an experience.

The route now goes east past the old Storsjön Chapel to Storsjön itself. This lake should not be confused with its much larger namesake 40km to the east (see below). The road follows the course of the Ljunga past numerous lakes full of salmon and red trout, and via Börtnan, Bergstjärn and Skålan to **Åsarna**, where it rejoins the main route.

78km Åsarna

Tännäs

The main route turns south-east at **Tännäs**, and follows the L312 along the southern shore of Lake Lossnen, which is full of fish. The road drops gently along the course of the Ljusna to **Hede** (population 1,200; altitude 420m). Hede has a church and a market, and is the focal point for a large, thinly populated area. A small road goes off to Råndalen across the mountains to the south. They rise to over 1,300m, and have been turned into the Sånfjället National Park. They are the habitat of elk and lynx, and also of brown bears.

62km Hede

The route continues eastwards along the L312, and after Hedeviken turns left onto the L315. At Vemdalen (altitude 320m) there is an interesting octagonal rococo church. The road then climbs steeply over Vemdalsskalet (altitude 720m) — a pass that goes through the middle of the Klövsjö Mountains. (There is a short cut to Åsarna along the L316, but this is very steep and is not recommended.) The L315 eventually arrives at **Rätansbyn** in the valley of the Ljunga. Here the route turns sharply north again along the R81, which runs through a glorious valley full of forests and lakes to the village of **Åsarna**.

64km Rätans-byn

41km Åsarna

The road now enters the province of Jämtland. Jämtland is

Frösö Church

almost completely covered by forests, and its economy is based on forestry. The main problem is transport: the rivers often form waterfalls or rapids, making them unsuitable for transporting timber. These obstacles then have to be bypassed by canals or by wooden troughs that the logs can slide down. The few towns that there are were not able to grow until the railways came, providing transport links to Norway and southern Sweden.

The R81 continues northwards, and at Svenstavik it reaches the southern tip of Storsjön. It runs along the spit of land between Storsjön and Lake Näkten to **Hackås**. Hackås has a particularly interesting old church, parts of which go back to when Christianity first came to these parts in the eleventh century. The interior contains some lovely old Romanesque frescos next to some more modern wall paintings. Next to the church is an old wooden bell tower. Thirty minutes' walk away is Hoverberget, where there is a lookout tower affording a marvellous view.

The R81 turns east and passes the northern shore of yet another lake called Locknesjön. The route then goes north again along the E75, which soon arrives at **Östersund** (population 54,000; altitude 298m). The capital of Jämtland is picturesquely situated on a slope above Storsjön, opposite the small island of Frösö. The town centre still has a large number of old wooden houses. Also of interest is the museum in Rådhusgatan. Just

78km
Öster-
sund

The Tännfors Falls

outside the town is the Jamtli open-air museum, which is one of the largest in Sweden, and contains a lovely old village. It is the site for an annual costume festival, which includes a traditional country wedding.

 The fertile island of **Frösö** is also very interesting. It is named after Frös, the old Norse god of fertility (*frö* is still the Swedish word for seed). The island is reached via a road bridge, next to which is a fine eleventh-century runestone with cross symbols on it. The road goes on up to Östberget (468m), from which there is a magnificent panorama of the lake with its steep, forest-covered shores. 6km further on is an old church going back to the twelfth century, which has been rebuilt in the Baroque style. Next to it is a free-standing bell tower, which is supported on twelve columns.

Cross-route to Trondheim in Norway

Öster-
sund
The E75 goes east from **Östersund** to the Norwegian border along a good, well-constructed road. 100km after Östersund, and just past Duved, there is a right turn along the L322. 10km along here via another side turning is the **Tännfors** — the most beautiful waterfall in Sweden to have been preserved in its natural state. Here the waters of the Indalsälv plunge vertically into Nornsjön over falls 60m across and 26m high.

Wintersports in Norrland

The E75 carries on eastwards, and crosses the border near 152km
Storlien. It continues a further 111km to **Trondheim**. The road Norwegian
remains good throughout, and has no steep hills. This route border
connects with the Arctic Road, which goes from Trondheim to the 111km
North Cape (see *The Visitor's Guide to Norway*). Trondheim

Öster-
sund

The main route leaves **Östersund** along the R88. It crosses the Indalsälv near Lit, and continues through the endless forests of Jämtland. It crosses the L341 at the lovely lakeside village of Hammerdal, and carries on to **Strömsund** (population 18,000; altitude 288m). Strömsund is a centre for the processing of talc and soapstone. The town lies in a narrow part of a long valley called Ströms vattudal. The Faxälv, the river that runs through it, has been dammed in various places to form a 160km long chain of lakes that extends all the way back to the Norwegian border.

101km
Ström-
sund

The R88 ends at Strömsund, and the route continues north-eastwards along the L343 through a landscape of lakes and forests. 21km further on is the village of **Lövberga**, which is situated at the southern end of Flasjön.

21km
Löv-
berga

Cross-route to Norway

Löv-
berga

The L342 turns left at **Lövberga**, and runs for 40km along the shore of Flasjön. The road then becomes rough as the road climbs steeply over a pass to Bågede. It continues through the gorgeous lake scenery of Ströms vattudal (see above) to the border post of **Gäddede**. Over the border, it becomes the Norwegian Road 74, which meets the Arctic Road near **Grong** in the area of Namsos (see *The Visitor's Guide to Norway*).

131km
Gäddede
105km
Grong

Löv-
berga

The main route continues from **Lövberga** along the L343. In the area of Hoting it passes through a 30km wide strip of the province of Ångermanland. This area is very fertile, and the ripening period is remarkably short. All the crops become ripe for harvest within a period of 2 to 3 months in the summer, thanks to the long hours of daylight and the unusual warmth of the short summer season.

At Hälleström the road crosses into the vast, thinly populated province of Lapland, which is the most northerly province in Sweden. The next place is **Dorotea** on the Bergevattena. Then at Meselefors the road and the railway together cross a bridge over the Ångermanälv, which is a marvellous river for anglers. The L343 follows the river as far as **Vilhelmina** (population 9,000; altitude 345m), which is sandwiched between Volgsjön and Baksjön, just beyond the junction with the L351. Its somewhat unusual name, like that of Dorotea to the south, comes from Queen Vilhelmina-Dorotea, who was consort to Gustav IV Adolf.

54km
Dorotea

60km
Vil-
helmina

The L343 goes on from Vilhelmina through continuous forests, occasionally interrupted by small areas of cultivated land. It

passes through Skarvsjöby and arrives at **Stensele**, where it 80km
Stensele
meets the E79 (Blåvägen — 'the Blue Road') from Umeå to Mo i
Rana.

Cross-route to Mo i Rana in Norway

This route goes left at **Stensele** along the E79 (Blåvägen) Stensele
through Storuman, and along past the lake of the same name. It 125km
carries on through wild mountain scenery to **Tärnaby**. Tärnaby is Tärnaby
a centre for walking tours into the surrounding mountains — Norra
Storfjället, for example. Tärnaby has recently become well-known
as a skiing centre. The two skiing stars Ingemar Stenmark and
Stig Strand both come from here. Although the Norwegian border
is 80km further up the road, the Swedish customs post is at 120km
Tärnaby. **Mo i Rana** is a further 40km beyond the border (see Mo i
Rana
The Visitor's Guide to Norway).

The main route follows the E79 from **Stensele** to **Storuman**, Stensele
then turns north-east again along the L343. It runs parallel to the
railway through a landscape of forests and swamps. It carries on 79km
past numerous lakes via Blattnicksele to **Sorsele**. Sorsele

Excursion to Ammarnäs

(180km there and back)

There is a left turn at Sorsele along a good, well-made road, which
follows the shore of Lake Storvindeln and the course of the
Vindelälv to the new tourist centre of **Ammarnäs**. Until recently,
this small village at the foot of a 1,600m high massif was inhabited
only by Lapps and crofters. But now it has been turned into a
large holiday centre, with hotels, chalets and a camping site. In
the summer it is a paradise for anglers and hill-walkers, and in the
winter a well-appointed ski resort. But equally attractive to
tourists are the Lapp handicrafts and the many other by-products
of the local economy: the meat, skins and antlers of the reindeer,
and delicacies such as red trout in the many different forms in
which it is served.

The L343 turns east from **Sorsele**, and continues through Sorsele
spruce forests that become increasingly sparse. The trees have
very short horizontal branches, and grow very tall and narrow.

This is due to the short growing period and the weight of the snow during the long, cold winters. The trees grow at about half the normal rate, and are about 80 to 100 years old before they are ready for felling. The road arrives at **Slagnäs**, where it crosses the Skellefteälv.

33km
Slagnäs

Detour via Arjeplog
(169km Slagnäs to Arvidsjaur)

Slagnäs

There is a left turn at **Slagnäs** along a side road, which goes north through a whole medley of lakes and wild forests. It passes through Gasa and along the shore of Lake Storavan, and then via Brännäs to the shores of Uddjaure (*jaure* is a Lapp word meaning lake). Here it turns right towards **Arjeplog**. Arjeplog has a museum with a display of old Lapp silverwork. It is situated on a narrow strip of land between Uddjaure and Lake Hornavan, the latter being the deepest lake in Sweden (221m). Arjeplog is on the L375, which goes north-west towards the Norwegian border (see below). But the present detour goes south-east along the L375, which comes down through dense forests to the small town of **Arvidsjaur**.

81km
Arjeplog

⌘

88km
Arvids-
jaur

Slagnäs
46km
Arvids-
jaur

The main route goes direct from **Slagnäs** along the L343 via Arvaviken to **Arvidsjaur** (population 8,000; altitude 388m). Arvidsjaur is primarily a centre for timber transport. There is an interesting open-air museum next to the church. There is also a Lapp settlement complete with tents and wooden huts, which the Lapps use when they stay here for religious festivals. But the settlement is naturally a tourist attraction too.

⌘

Cross-route to Bodø in Norway

Arvids-
jaur

Arvidsjaur is at the south-eastern end of the L375 Silvervägen (Silver Road), which goes north-west across the border into Norway. It goes across a vast, empty plateau with forests, bogs and lakes. From **Arjeplog** (see above) it runs along the shore of Uddjaure. It then climbs gradually via Jutis, Jäkkvik and Lillviken, and along the north-western shore of Sädvajaure. On Graddisfjället it crosses the border and its name changes to Graddisveien. It descends through Junkerdalen past a well-known tourist centre. 20km further on near Storjord it enters the E6 Arctic Road (Norway's main north–south artery), and connects

88km
Arje-
plog
139km
Norwegian
border

with routes to **Bodø** and the North Cape (see *The Visitor's Guide to Norway*).

152km
Bodø

From **Arvidsjaur** the L343 turns north again, and winds through heavily forested hills, past lakes, bogs and fast-flowing streams. Near Moskosel it crosses the Abmoälv, which is closely followed by the Piteälv. Soon after Norden, the L374 comes in from Piteå (see page 155), while the L343 continues ever northwards. The rocks covered in moss and the extensive forests of stunted birches are signs that the Arctic Circle is near. The road crosses it just past the small village of Vajmat.

Arvids-
jaur

   A short way further on, the road arrives at the old Lapp market centre of **Jokkmokk** (population 3,200). Jokkmokk is the only place on this route where the nomadic Lapps can still be seen during the summer months. There are about 10,000 Lapps in Sweden, most of whom have become permanently settled. They are seldom more than 1.6m (5ft 3in) tall, have their own language and wear brightly coloured clothing; they are renowned for their peaceable temperament (see page 15). Jokkmokk still has a reindeer market in February, and the division of the reindeer takes place here in the autumn. The Lapps also use Jokkmokk for their traditional tribal meetings. In the centre of the town are a sixteenth-century Lapp church made of wood and a special Lapp school. The Lapp Museum is also interesting. The midnight sun shines here for 3 weeks from 12 June to 3 July. There are many interesting things to see in the surrounding area. The town lies on the Lilla Luleälv, which in several places forms rapids and waterfalls.

159km
Jokk-
mokk

Cross-route to Narvik in Norway

This route goes north from **Jokkmokk** along the R97, and runs parallel to the railway as it passes through the lake region of Vajkijaur. Further north, both the road and railway follow the course of the Stora Luleälv. To the right is the massive **Harsprånget** power station, which with an output of 350,000kW is one of the largest in Sweden. It obtains its power from the Stora Luleälv, which at one time plunged 80m within a distance of 2km, including a single vertical drop of 30m. A dam has now been built at the top of the falls, and most of the water is harnessed for the power station. But provided the water level is not too low, the falls are still fairly impressive. The previous water level is clearly

Jokk-
mokk

Harsprånget power station

46km
Porjus indicated by deep grooves in the banks either side.

The road crosses the Stora Luleälv and arrives at **Porjus**, where there is yet another hydroelectric power station. 6km beyond Porjus, a small road goes off to the left to the shore of Stora Lulevatten — a long, winding lake, famous for its salmon and pike. From Luspebryggen a boat runs the whole length of the lake, past the impressive cascades of Jaure Kaskafors, to **Stora Sjöfallet**, which is the largest waterfall in Sweden. The falls can also be seen from the rough road that runs along the shore, near to which there is also a camping site.

The R97 leaves the Stora Luleälv at Porjus, and turns northeast through a moderately hilly region with forests. To the right of the road is the **Muddus National Park** — a region of wild, untouched forests, where bears, lynxes and gluttons (the European equivalent of wolverines) are still to be found. Visitors are banned from the reserve from 15 March to 31 July.

53km
Gälli-
vare The next town is **Gällivare** (population 25,000; altitude 360m). Gällivare is an important junction on the Lapland Railway, with several small branches leading up to the local iron-ore mines of Malmberget (the name actually means 'the iron-ore mountain').

The Kiruna-Narvik iron-ore train

The ores are found in vertical seams under a mountain that consists mostly of gneiss. They are mined via underground shafts with considerable difficulty. A small side-road leads up from the town to Malmberget (12km there and back), which has an interesting mining museum. Guided tours underground can also be arranged. There are yet more iron mines at Koskullskulle, 4km further north.

After Gällivare the route turns left along the R98, which goes north, past many lakes full of fish, to **Svappavaara** (altitude 325m), which at one time was a thriving iron-mining community. But many people have left since the slump in the steel industry, and Svappavaara is gradually turning into a ghost town. There is an alternative cross-route from Svappavaara into Finland and Norway (see below).

80km
Svappa-
vaara

The R98 continues north-west from Svappavaara through a region of forests, swamps and lakes that is mostly inhabited by Finns and Lapps. It goes through Alttajärvi and arrives at **Kiruna** (population 30,000; altitude 500m), which is the centre of Sweden's best-known mining area. The most northerly town in Sweden, it is situated at the southern end of Luossajärvi (*järvi* is the Finnish word for lake). Up to a century ago, it was no more than a small Lapp settlement, but has since grown into a large

48km
Kiruna

complex of modern developments. Half the mines are state-owned while half are privately owned. Kiruna has not been immune from the slump in the demand for Swedish ores. The closing of some mines has meant that miners have had to leave, some of whom were once the highest-paid workers in the world.

To the south of the town is the famous iron-ore mountain, which is split in two by a vast open-cast mine. However, most of the mining is done underground. Most of the ore is transported by rail on the famous iron-ore line to the Norwegian port of Narvik. But a small amount is shipped from the Swedish port of Luleå during the few months when the Gulf of Bothnia is free of ice. Guided tours can be arranged round some of the mines.

From Kiruna it is possible to visit **Kebnekaise** (altitude 2,123m), the highest mountain in Sweden, which can be climbed by well-equipped climbers with the help of a guide (information available from the tourist office).

166km
Narvik

The R98 continues north-west from Kiruna, and eventually crosses the Norwegian border to **Narvik**, where it connects with the E6 Arctic Road (see *The Visitor's Guide to Norway*).

Cross-route into Norway via Finland

Svappa-
vaara
23km
Vittangi

This route goes the same way as the previous cross-route from Jokkmokk as far as **Svappavaara** (see above). But at Svappavaara it turns east along the L395 to **Vittangi** (247m), which is situated by the Torneälv at a point where it broadens out into a lake.

The route turns due north along the L396, which runs straight through an area of continuous forest inhabited only by elk and other game. The dense, almost primaeval forest is frequently interspersed by lakes. Travellers are advised to take great care when walking off the road, as the land is often very boggy. After 20km the road passes a small settlement of Lapps and Finns called Sappisaasi. It later crosses a lake called Vuoksujärvi, and meets the small settlement of Soppero on the opposite shore.

100km
Kares-
uando
(Finnish
border)

The road continues through wild, uninhabited forests, with occasional small settlements, until it arrives at the border village of **Karesuando**, which has the most northerly church in Sweden. It also has the lowest average temperature in Sweden (26°F). But there is no need to worry, as in July and August it can even be hot! At Karesuando the road crosses the Finnish border, which at this point is formed by a river — the Muonioälv in Swedish or Muoniojoki in Finnish. (See *The Visitor's Guide to Finland*).

The route turns left into the E78 — the Finnish Road 21 — which it follows north-westwards along the course of the river. In several places the river broadens out into a lake, and the road occasionally passes an isolated Lapp settlement. It eventually arrives at the **Kilpisjärvi** tourist station. This stands on the shore of a good fishing lake of the same name, and at the foot of a strangely shaped mountain called **Saanantunturi** (1,024m), which is the sacred mountain of the Lapps.

8km along the lakeshore is the Norwegian border (Siilastupa), where the customs formalities are very few. The E78 now descends via Helligskogen along the course of the Skibotnelv, which is famous in Norway for its salmon. Just before **Skibotn** the road enters the E6 Arctic Road, which runs along the shore of the beautiful Lyngenfjord, with its strikingly green waters. At this point the route connects with the Arctic tour of Norway (see *The Visitor's Guide to Norway*).

110km
Kilpis
-järvi

8km
Norwegian
border
40km
Skibotn

From **Jokkmokk** the main route turns south-east along the R97. This good, fast road follows the course of the Lilla Luleälv, and after 12km crosses south of the Arctic Circle again. It descends alongside this very fast-flowing river, which after 40km combines with the Stora Luleälv. The confluence is followed by an impressive set of rapids. The most famous of these used to be the Porsifors, over which the river dropped 25m within the space of 1.8km. But unfortunately the harnessing of much of the water for hydroelectricity has led to serious environmental damage.

Jokk-
mokk

The road carries on, with occasional glimpses of the roaring river to the left, to **Edefors**, where the road crosses the Luleälv. There is a view of the mighty Edefors rapids, where the river drops 22m over a distance of 3km. 28km further on, just past the village of Övere Svartlå, the road enters the Boden military zone (see page 192). For the next 40km, all foreigners are subject to strict regulations: they are forbidden to leave the road or take photographs, and must always carry passports for identification purposes. The town of **Boden** itself is an important railway junction and airforce base.

70km
Ede-
fors

68km
Boden

15km south-east of Boden, the R97 leaves the restricted military zone. The next place of interest is the lovely old village of Gammelstad, where an ancient people's council or *thing* used to assemble. The fifteenth-century church has a lovely Flemish

Luleå

altar. It is surrounded by a settlement of 400 little wooden houses, known as a *kyrkestad*, where church-goers from a wide area around used to stay overnight.

40km
Luleå

It is only another 5km to the city of **Luleå** (population 68,000). Luleå is situated by the Gulf of Bothnia, and is a major port for the shipment of iron-ores from the mining regions of Kiruna and Gällivare. The harbour is frozen up for 6 or 7 months of the year, during which time all the ores have to be shipped from Narvik on the ice-free Norwegian coast. The city is a very old one, but very few of the old buildings are left. The plush modern centre shows some of the advantages of this. There is also an interesting museum of Lapp art and culture.

From Luleå the route first crosses the mouth of the Luleälv, and then turns south into the E4, which comes down from Haparanda on the Finnish border. The E4 runs near to the irregular coastline of the Gulf of Bothnia — the northern extension of the Baltic that divides Sweden from Finland. This part of it is known in Swedish as Bottenviken or Bottniska viken. At first the road stays mostly out of sight of the sea. But after Rosvik it runs along the shore between the forest and the sea to the village of Öjebyn, with its lovely old church.

River-rafting in Lapland

5km away is the old port of **Piteå**, which is partly located on the island of **Häggholm**, and is surrounded by some fine bathing resorts. In spite of its northerly location, it boasts the best sunshine records and the highest sea temperatures in Sweden! There are two possible routes out of Piteå. One option is the route across the island of Häggholm, followed by a ferry across the Pitsund and back to the E4. The alternative is to go back to Öjebyn and cross the Berviksund to Berviken via the E4 bridge.

53km
Piteå

The E4 continues southwards, mostly out of sight of the coast, to the industrial port of **Skellefteå** (population 72,000). The chief industry here is the refining of metal ores from the nearby mining area of Boliden. Of particular interest are the *kyrkestad* (see above) and the museum at Bonnstan.

88km
Skell-
efteå

⌘

Detour via Norsjö and Lycksele
(298km Skellefteå to Umeå)
This detour is about twice as long as the direct route to Umeå (see below), and goes through the interior of the province of Västerbotten. It is intended in particular for travellers who are returning along this coast from a tour of Norway or Finland, and

who wish to gain an impression of the interior of northern Sweden.

Skell-
efteå
The route goes west from **Skellefteå** along the L369, which runs along the north bank of the Skellefteälv through a populous industrial area. At Finnfors, 33km along the road, there is a turning to the right for the mining area of **Boliden**, which was discovered in the 1920s. The ores mined there include those of copper, silver, gold and lead. Visitors who are especially interested may care to make the 14km detour to see some of the world's most up-to-date mines.

86km
Norsjö
The L369 continues westwards through a more thinly populated region of forests and lakes via Bastuträsk to **Norsjö** (population 10,000; altitude 291m). Norsjö is a popular skiing resort, and is prettily situated on the shore of Norsjön. The route skirts the north shore of the lake, and turns left into the R90.

A short way further on, a side-road leads off to the zinc-and lead-mining area of Högkulla, which is about 10km to the north of the main road. There are two attractions on the way to Högkulla. The first is a beautiful waterfall called the Långselefors, which has so far been spared the ravages of a hydroelectric scheme. Then the road crosses underneath the Linbana — a 100km long cable railway that links the two mining districts of Boliden and Kristineberg, together with numerous mines in between. Visitors must return to the R90 along the same route.

The R90 goes south-westwards past the shore of Lake Kvammarn, and continues through a hilly region of forests and lakes. It crosses the Vindelälv and eventually arrives at **Lyck-**
83km
Lyck-
sele
sele (population 14,000; altitude 218m). Lycksele is an important market centre in southern Lapland, and is often known as the Stockholm of the Lapps. The Lapp settlement is of particular interest. The Lapps use it for accommodation when they come in to market or to church. Lycksele also has the most northerly zoo in Europe.

The route turns south-east along the E79 (Blåvägen or Blue Road), which descends along the course of the Umeälv. The Umeälv is an important river for the transport of timber. It sometimes broadens out into a lake, and sometimes runs in a fast, raging torrent. The landscape either side consists of hills covered in dense forests. After 65km the road arrives at
65km
Granön
Granön, which is a popular centre for anglers. The Umeälv is famous for its salmon, which can be seen climbing the salmon ladders that are built to help the fish overcome obstacles such as waterfalls or dams.

The E79 carries on south-eastwards. It leaves the course of the river for a while, and then returns to it near Vännäs in the more populous region that borders the coast. Soon after that, the Vindelälv enters the Umeälv. The E79 continues via Brännland to **Umeå** (see below).

64km
Umeå

The main route continues southwards on the E4 from **Skellefteå** along the somewhat flatter coastal plain. The sea is mostly hidden by the dense forests that go right up to the shore. The road passes a ruined abbey at Bureå. Lävånger is beautifully situated on an inlet called Gärdviken, and has an old church surrounded by a *kyrkestad* (see page 154).

Skell-
efteå

⌘

The road carries on down the coast via Bygdeå to the old city of **Umeå** (population 75,000). Umeå was founded in 1622, and is the capital of the province of Västerbotten. There was severe fighting in this area during the Finnish War of 1808–9, when the Russians advanced on Umeå across the ice of the Gulf of Bothnia. The local handicrafts include some marvellous silverwork. Umeå has had its own university since 1965. Of particular interest is the Gammlia open-air museum, which is in a park to the north of the city. It includes some old historical buildings and a museum of Lapp culture. The city depends for its livelihood on the Umeälv. 10 million metres of timber are floated down river from distances of up to 200km, and are then loaded onto ships at Umeå. The river is also important for hydro-electricity, with fifteen power stations providing power for the surrounding areas. The power station at Storrhorrfors to the west of the town is the biggest hydroelectric plant in Western Europe, with a capacity of 375,000kW. Umeå is also a ferry port, with passenger services to Vaasa in Finland (see *The Visitor's Guide to Finland*).

144km
Umeå

⌘

The E4 continues in a straight line south from Umeå through a mostly flat landscape, and leaves Västerbotten for the province of Ångermanland. It soon arrives at the old port of **Nordmaling** (population 8,000). Nordmaling used to be important at one time, but has since been overtaken by other ports which are more favourably situated in relation to the industrial hinterland. The lovely old fourteenth-century church bears witness to its illustrious past.

60km
Nord-
maling

⌘

The E4 carries on along the coast to **Örnsköldvik** (population 60,000), which is situated on an inlet of the same name.

55km
Örns-
köldvik

Lapland's Staloluokta Church

This part of the coast is again important for the trans-shipment of timber. The road now runs at some distance from the coast, but there are numerous side-roads to bathing resorts along one of the most beautiful stretches of the Swedish coastline. After about 35km, the road runs closer to the coast, offering several magnificent views of the many inlets and skerries.

82km
Sandö

At **Sandö** the road crosses a 47m high bridge over the fjord-like mouth of the Ångermanälv, which together with its tributaries has come down the whole length of the province from across the Norwegian border. It is one of many rivers that cross Sweden from north-west to south-east, and without which the Swedish timber trade would never have been viable. The Ångermanälv is navigable to ships for about 50km inland.

36km
Härnö-
sand

The E4 carries on through a more populous region, sometimes running directly along the coast. The next town is **Härnösand** (population 27,000), which is the capital both of the province of Ångermanland and of the administrative region of Västernorrlands län. The coastal region south of Härnösand is heavily industrialised. The industries include the processing of timber that comes down the Indalsälv, plus a variety of chemical industries. The road crosses the Indalsälv near Bergeforsen, where it forms rapids that have been partially harnessed for hydroelectricity.

The road soon arrives at the modern industrial port of **Sundsvall** (population 95,000), which is again an important centre for the trans-shipment of timber, with a large number of wood-based industries. The E4 continues southwards at some distance from the coast through a region which, though heavily forested, is more densely populated than is usual for Sweden. It soon crosses into the province of Hälsingland, and runs past numerous lakes and rivers covered from bank to bank with floating logs.

60km Sundsvall

The next town of **Hudiksvall** (population 20,000) again depends for its livelihood on the processing and trans-shipment of the timber that is brought down into the bay (the Hudiksvallfjärd). The E4 continues due south, mostly at some distance from the irregular coastline. It frequently has to cross fjords, estuaries or inlets — for example, at the small industrial town of **Iggesund**, which is sandwiched between Iggesjön and the sea. The further away the road goes from the sea, the more dense the forests become.

89km Hudiks-vall

10km Igge-sund

The E4 rejoins the coast near the industrial port of **Söderhamn** (population 32,000). Like many of the ports along this coast, Söderhamn owes its early development to the achievements of Gustav II Adolf, who in 1617 won a long-standing war with the Russians, and thus established firm possession of a large portion of the Swedish coast. The E4 continues close to the sea along a flat coastal plain that is thinly populated and often marshy. At this stage it runs parallel to the railway.

60km Söder-hamn

The next important town is **Gävle** (population 85,000), which is the capital of the province of Gästrikland. It is also the main port for the shipping of timber and ores from the nearby mining regions. Very little is left of the old parts of the town. The ancient royal castle was also replaced by a palace in the seventeenth century (this now houses the local government headquarters). Visitors will be surprised to discover that Gävle is the site of the most northerly coffee-roasting factory in Europe. The Swedes, like the Germans, have made coffee their national drink, in the same way that the British traditionally prefer tea. (See also page 115.)

93km Gävle

The route leaves the E4, turning eastwards along the R76, which follows the coast. It passes through the village of Järvsta,

⚘ where a vast number of prehistoric discoveries have been made, including a stone circle in the shape of a ship. Just past Skutsär the road crosses the Dalälv, which like other rivers further north is important for transporting timber from the interior. After the turning for Älvkarleby, there is another right turn along a small road signposted to Marma. The route follows this road, which goes south again away from the coast. The road runs along the bank of the Dalälv, which at this point has broadened out into a lake. After Marma the route rejoins the E4 in the area of Mehedeby.

55km   The E4 continues southwards through an area of forests and
Tierp   swamps. A little further on there is a turning for **Tierp**, with its
⚘ fascinating fourteenth-century church. It has some lovely frescos inside, and a thirteenth-century bell tower. The road passes the ancient abbey of Husborgsby on the left. 30km to the east of the main road is the iron-mining area of Dannemora, which has produced high-quality ores since the fifteenth century. At Läby there is a left turn for the village of Vendel (10km), where some fascinating prehistoric remains have been found in the
⚘ churchyard. This is a region full of ancient sites and remains from all periods of Scandinavian history — from old churches and castles to runestones and grave mounds. It was indeed the cradle of Scandinavian civilisation. For there is something of interest in practically every village in an area which is centred on Uppsala — Sweden's oldest cultural centre.

59km   The E4 becomes very straight, and continues past the ancient
Uppsala site of Gamla Uppsala towards the old university town of **Upp-**
77km   **sala** (see page 113). The route leaves Uppsala along the E4
Stock- motorway to **Stockholm** (see page 37), and thus returns to the
holm   point where it first started.

Åre village, Jämtland

Lapp chapel, Jämtland

Vadstena Castle, on the Göta Canal

6 THE GÖTA CANAL

Sweden's Most Beautiful Waterway

The Göta Canal is the waterway that links Sweden's two largest cities, Göteborg and Stockholm. It thus forms the shortest shipping route from the Baltic Sea to the Skagerrak and thence to the North Sea. This waterway runs through the heart of Sweden through some really delightful scenery.

It is in fact made up of several canals. The first section is the Trollhättan Canal, which runs parallel to the Götaälv from Göteborg to Vänersborg on Lake Vänern. It passes the famous falls at Trollhättan, and climbs by means of several locks. The route then crosses Sweden's largest lake to the next section of the canal, which runs from Sjötorp to Karlsborg on Lake Vättern. The canal again climbs via numerous locks to a maximum height of 91.5m on Lake Viken, which is one of several natural waterways that form parts of this section of the canal. The route crosses Lake Vättern to Motala, and the canal descends again through several lakes. It eventually reaches sea level near Söderköping, where it enters a long Baltic inlet called Slätbaken. The route then continues past the Baltic islands and skerries to Stockholm.

The waterway passes through a total of sixty-five locks, of which sixteen are along the 22km long section between Lake Boren and Lake Roxen. The total length of the waterway is 596km, of which only 190km is made up of actual canal. The pleasure steamers that ply the route normally take 3 days to complete the journey, with two overnight stops. But between May and July it is possible to travel the whole way by daylight, in which case 4 days are required. There are between nine and twelve sailings a month during the peak season (from June to August).

The canal has a long history. The major part of the route from Lake Vänern to the Baltic was built by Count von Platten during the period between 1810 and 1832. Since then only a few minor alterations have been made. The canal thus has a delightful air of

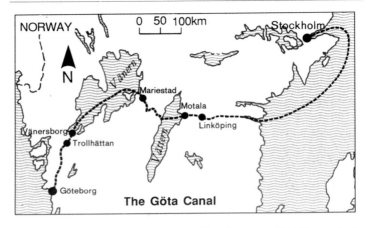

The Göta Canal

old-fashioned grace. The locks are like those on British canals in that members of the boat crews must provide help in opening and closing the lock gates. The canal also goes through some marvellous scenery.

The canal is not limited to travellers on the official passenger routes. It is also open to private craft such as yachts and motor boats. The maximum dimensions allowed are 32m in length and 7m in width, with a maximum draught of 2.82m. The maximum allowed mast height is 24m above water level. Canal users must pay a toll at the first tollbooth along the route. The tollbooths not only provide full information in English on canal regulations, but also sell maps and other navigational aids. The maximum speed permitted along the canal is 4.8kn or 9km/h.

Cabin berths are available on the official passenger steamers. Prices for these vary depending on the level of comfort required. A coupon for meals (without drinks) can be obtained on deck and children under 6 may travel free, while those between 6 and 12 may travel half price apart from the cost of a berth. Early booking is highly recommended. Deck tickets are available for sections of the route, while cabin berths can only be booked for the whole journey.

There is no way of taking motor vehicles aboard. However, special arrangements can be made to transfer cars separately between Göteborg and Stockholm. They are transported overland so as to be available for collection at the end of the journey, the cost of which includes insurance. But it is both easier and cheaper to book a combined boat and rail ticket, so that one can

Part of the Göta Canal

then return to the starting point by train.

The boats leave Göteborg from the quay next to Lilla Bommens torg at the north-eastern end of the city centre. They dock in Stockholm on the island of Riddarholmen in the city centre. Further details on bookings are available from the Swedish National Tourist Office (see page 233).

The Route
The embarkation point at **Göteborg** (see page 96) is the quay alongside Lilla Bommens torg, which can be reached via the E3 from outside the city, or via Östra Hamngatan from the city centre. The departure time is 9am.

Göteborg

Bohus Castle ruins

The first section of the route is the **Trollhättan Canal**. This runs mostly along the course of the Götaälv, apart from cuts which have been made to bypass weirs and falls. This section of the route was originally built in the seventeenth and eighteenth centuries, but it has since been widened to accommodate smaller seagoing vessels. The areas bordering the Götaälv are important industrially, and the river has been harnessed to supply them with the necessary electrical power.

20km from Göteborg, near the industrial town of Kungälv, the canal passes the old castle of **Bohus**, which gave its name to the province of Bohuslän. After Kungälv it enters the green valley of the Götaälv. The massive locks at Lilla Edet, Trollhättan and Brinkebergskulle raise the canal level to 44.4m above sea level. The canal also passes under the Stallbacka Bridge, which with a length of 1.4km and a height of 27m is the largest bridge over any lake in Sweden. As the boat passes through the locks at **Trollhättan**, there are views of the enormous power station that uses the water from the famous Trollhättan Falls (see page 94).

In the late afternoon the boat arrives at **Vänersborg**, where it enters Lake Vänern. **Lake Vänern** (see page 127) is Sweden's

20km
Bohus

84km
Väners-
borg

largest lake. It forms a vital transport link from the industrial areas
of Karlsborg in the north and Lidköping in the south via the
Trollhättan Canal to Göteborg. Several other important canals run
into the lake, such as the **Dalsland Canal**, which goes west
into Norway, and the **Säffle Canal**, which goes north into the
province of Värmland. Lake Vänern is full of interesting boats,
including both merchant and sports vessels. The steamer route
passes a number of lovely islands. Of these, Kållandsö is the
setting for the beautiful **Läckö Castle**, which is visible from a
long distance away, while Lurö has a ruined abbey, and the Eken
archipelago includes fifteen bird sanctuaries.

122km
Sjötorp

The boat leaves the lake at **Sjötorp** just north of Mariestad,
where it enters the second section of the Göta Canal. In the long
days of midsummer, this is the only part of the first half of the
route where the canal is shrouded in darkness. The locks now
come thick and fast, there being as many as twenty within the
36km as far as Tårtorp. The only town along this section of the
canal is **Töreboda**, where it is crossed by both road and rail.
Töreboda also boasts the canal's smallest ferry. The price of the
twenty-second crossing is only 5 öre, and has remained so since
1919!

The canal reaches its highest point (about 92m) at Hajstorp.
36km
Tårtorp

Then at **Tårtorp** it enters the wild and beautiful **Lake Viken**.
After Lake Viken only one lock is needed (near Forsvik) to bring
the canal down to the level of Lake Vättern (89m). The boat
crosses Bottensjön, which is effectively part of Lake Vättern. The
entrance to the lake proper is guarded by the ancient fortress of
Karlsborg, which stands high on a peninsula. The boat is
Karls-
borg
timetabled to arrive here at 10.15am.

Lake Vättern is Sweden's second-largest lake. It is famous
for its clean, transparent waters and its large fish population. Like
Lake Vänern it is an important route for transporting timber.
During the 25km crossing from Karlsborg to Vadstena, the boat
passes numerous rafts of logs being towed by small tugs to the
southern end of the lake. The world-famous match factories at
Jönköping are not their only destination. At 2pm the boat arrives
25km
Vadstena
at the small medieval town of **Vadstena**, which is famous for its
abbey and its castle (see page 106).

The canal runs close to the lake shore from Vadstena to
Motala (see page 107). This final section of the canal from Lake
Motala
Vättern to the Baltic was completed in 1851. The Göta Canal is
owned by a private company called the Göta-Kanalbolag, which is

Final stages of the Göta journey — Stockholm Town Hall

based in Motala and is one of the oldest firms in Sweden. In Motala market place there is a statue of Count von Platten, the canal's founder. The canal continues parallel to the Motala River. It passes through six locks within the space of 4km between Motala and Lake Boren, dropping about 22m.

The 12km run along **Lake Boren** is one of the most delightful parts of the whole route. There are many lovely old castles and estates along the green banks of the lake. The canal leaves the lake at **Borensberg**. In the 22km section which follows, it drops from 68.5m to 32.5m, and passes through sixteen locks. Although the locks are rather old-fashioned, they usually work fairly quickly, and the boat never waits more than 15 minutes at each one. At Ljungsbro the canal crosses a road via the only aqueduct on the whole route.

At **Berg** the boat enters **Lake Roxen**. It is late evening by now, but the long days of midsummer should permit a magnificent view of the lake, with **Vreta Abbey** on the shore. The lake is 26km long, and the boat leaves it again at **Norsholm**. Two further locks at Bråtton and Hulta bring the canal down to a height of 28m before it runs into the tiny **Lake Asplången**. The boat continues through the night, passing through nine further locks,

16km
Borens-
berg

22km
Berg

26km
Nors-
holm

until it eventually arrives at **Söderköping**. This picturesque little medieval town is well-known as a spa on account of the healing properties of St Ragnhild's springs.

The boat leaves Söderköping in the early hours of the morning, and passes through a lock at the foot of a steep hill called Ramunderberg. Two further locks at Tegelbruket and Mem bring the canal down to sea level. The boat now runs along **Slätbaken** — an inlet from the Baltic where the sea comes a long way inland. On the south side of Slätbaken are the ruins of Gustav Vasa's mighty fortress at **Stegeborg**, with its 26m high tower.

The boat now leaves the canal well behind, and comes right out into the waters of the Baltic. It continues north-east along the coast, passing numerous inlets, wooded islands and skerries. Not far from Trosa and Tulgarn Castle, the boat turns north along a narrow inlet called the **Järnfjord**. Eventually, after a 175km run along the coast, the boat passes along a short canal to **Södertälje** (see page 84).

The final part of the voyage through Lake Mälaren takes only 3 hours. The boat runs past the islands to the west of Stockholm, including Drottningholm Castle, and eventually reaches its destination on the island of Riddarholmen, which is right in the centre of **Stockholm** (see page 37). Shortly before arrival, the boat passes the impressive tower of Stockholm Town Hall on the left.

Söder-
köping

⌘

175km
Söder-
tälje

39km
Stock-
holm

7 ADVICE TO TOURISTS

The information on the pages which follow is continually updated and revised to take account of changes in currency, prices, accommodation, etc. However, further changes are always liable to occur. Complete accuracy cannot, therefore, be guaranteed, and such information should be used for general guidance only.

1. Travel

Many potential visitors to Sweden are put off by the long journey. For unless one travels by air (see page 170), it involves either a long sea journey or a long land journey interspersed with ferries. A boat trip, however, can often prove the most relaxing way of beginning or ending a holiday. Moreover, sleeping on the boat overnight can save valuable time for visitors who are touring the country.

There are several different ways of travelling by ferry. The direct route from Britian is from Felixstowe or Newcastle to Göteborg. Alternatively, one can make the sea journey to a Dutch, German or Danish port, and then travel overland to meet one of the short ferry crossings between Denmark and Sweden. The shortest of these routes is from Helsingør to Helsingborg; but there are other possibilities — Grenå to Varberg, and Frederikshavn to Göteborg, to name but two. These routes are listed more fully on page 173.

Transport within Sweden itself is to a certain extent hampered by the long distances involved. But it has improved enormously in recent years, thanks to the modernisation of the road and rail networks, and the introduction of new internal air services.

The Swedish Rail Network

For British visitors to Sweden, there are rail routes from Victoria Station, London via Dover to Ostend or Liverpool Street Station via Harwich to Hook of Holland. It is also possible to use the sea route via Harwich-Esbjerg.

The railway system in Sweden developed early and quickly, encouraged by the long distances which people had to travel. Today the network comprises about 12,000km of line, or 15km of line per 10,000 inhabitants — the highest proportion for any country in Europe. The majority of the network has been electrified, including all the major routes.

There are three categories of train in Sweden: express trains, through trains and local trains. The express trains are extremely fast, covering the 456km between Stockholm and Göteborg in about four hours. Customers may travel either first class or second class. The carriages are modern and in good condition. Trains on the longer routes are well supplied with sleeper carriages. These are mostly filled with convertible compartments that can be transformed into seating compartments during the daytime. The longer routes also provide good, modern dining car facilities.

The cost per kilometre becomes less the further one travels. It is therefore advisable to book a ticket right through to the final destination. Return fares are about 20 per cent cheaper than single fares, but are only available on journeys of over 50km each way. Children under 6 may travel free, while those between 6 and 12 may travel half-price. Travellers on express trains, and on some of the other long-distance trains, must also buy a seat reservation. The Swedish State Railways (*Svenska Statens Järnvägar* or SJ) offer reductions for families, tourists, travellers over 67 years old, and party bookings. There are also special concessions for round trips, which can be broken off at any point during the journey. Up-to-date information about prices and services available can be obtained from the Swedish National Tourist Office (see page 233).

Bus and Coach Travel

For British travellers, there are several coach routes to Sweden, including London to Stockholm, to Göteborg, to Malmö and from Harwich to Stockholm. The Swedish State Railways provide a number of long-distance coach services, most of these during the summer. They are only to be found on longer routes such as from Stockholm to Malmö or to places in the north. There are several private companies that run coach services to tourist areas. Northern Sweden is also well served by post buses, which cover a

Arlanda Airport

total road network of about 9,000km. One of the most fascinating of these routes is the Via Lappia from Umeå to Mo i Rana in Norway. Another interesting possibility is to combine an air flight to northern Sweden with trips along the post-bus network. Further information about all these services can be obtained from the Swedish Post Office (address: Post Stürelsen, Diligenzsektionen, S-10500 Stockholm), or from the Swedish National Tourist Office (see page 233).

Air Travel

There are many international flights to Göteborg and Stockholm and flights to Copenhagen in Denmark, or to Stavanger or Oslo in Norway with connections to Sweden. Travellers are advised to contact their Tourist office or Travel Agent for further details. The Scandinavian Air System (SAS) provides internal flights between Sweden's twenty-three passenger airports, which are within easy reach of the country's 150 main towns. Stockholm has two airports, of which Arlanda handles all international traffic, plus most internal lines, while some of the internal flights go from the smaller airport at Bromma. Both airports are some distance from the city centre, but are linked to it by a fast and frequent airport bus service. Different operating companies offer a variety of

Most highways in Sweden are fast and quiet

reductions on charter flights. They also provide a number of special flights to the far north, especially during the period of the midnight sun. The internal air network is well developed to serve the transport needs of this far-flung country. Apart from passenger and freight lines, there are provisions for medical and rescue services. There are also opportunities for individual passengers to arrange private 'air-taxi' flights.

Car Travel in Sweden

In 1967, Sweden took the final drastic step of swapping from driving on the left to driving on the right. This measure was difficult and expensive, but brought Sweden in line with all other countries in continental Europe. Britain and Ireland are the only remaining European countries that drive on the left, and were thus the only countries not to benefit from this change.

In the past, many Swedish roads were still unsurfaced, but this is thankfully no longer the case. Apart from a few fast-disappearing exceptions, all roads in Sweden are fully made up, and most highways are broad and well surfaced. Only one or two

Layby with a view

main routes remain unmetalled in the far north. But the well-kept gravel surfaces are given a thorough overhaul every spring after the ravages of winter frost. Signposting is good throughout. International routes (E-roads) are indicated by green signs with a white border. Trunk routes each have a two-figure number preceded by an R (= *riksväg*), while other main roads have a three-figure number preceded by an L (= *länsväg*).

Although the main roads are good and fast, drivers are subject to severe speed restrictions. The speed limit in built-up areas is 50km/h (31mph), while it varies on country roads between 70km/h (43mph) and 90km/h (56mph). Only on motorways and certain other main routes is a maximum of 110km/h (68mph) allowed. (For other traffic regulations see page 175.) But in spite of these restrictions, it is possible to achieve a good average speed on most main roads, where, because traffic is light, constant speeds are possible over long distances. A relatively low maximum speed also makes for savings in petrol consumption, which is useful in areas where petrol stations are few and far between. However, travellers in such areas are still advised to take a sizeable spare can of petrol.

All Scandinavian countries place severe restrictions on drinking and driving. The maximum permitted alcohol level is very low, and drivers exceeding this limit are subject to severe penalties.

Travellers will be pleasantly surprised to find so many car parks and lay-bys at the roadside. There is often a kiosk, together with a shelter and a picnic area with tables and seats.

Ferry Routes to Sweden

A long ferry journey can sometimes prove expensive, especially if a car or caravan is included. It is possible to reduce such costs by choosing shorter ferry routes and travelling overland across Germany, Denmark, or maybe even Holland. But this alternative is costly in terms of time. A long sea trip, on the other hand, not only saves time on an overnight crossing, but can also be a relaxing way of beginning or ending a holiday. The pros and cons in each case will depend on the individual. But whatever route one chooses, it is highly advisable to book well in advance to avoid disappointment.

The table below gives information not only about ferries to Sweden, but also about other ferry services that may be of use, either as stepping stones on the way or for those who wish to travel on to Finland as well. It is not possible to provide details of prices and timetables, since these vary enormously according to season. Such detailed information can be obtained from travel agents or from the Swedish National Tourist Office.

Ferry Routes to Sweden

Route	Shipping Companies	Frequency and Duration
Britain to Sweden direct		
Felixstowe to Göteborg	Sessan Tor Line	3-4/week (25hr)
Newcastle to Göteborg	Sessan Tor Line	weekly (26hr)
	DFDS	2 weekly (26hr)
Harwich to Göteborg	DFDS	3 weekly (23hr)
Britain to Denmark		
Harwich to Esbjerg	DFDS	daily (20hr)
Newcastle to Esbjerg	DFDS	3/week (22hr)

Germany to Denmark

| Puttgarden to Rødbyhavn | DB/DSB | 35/day (1hr) |

Germany to Sweden

| Travemünde to Trelleborg | TT Saga Line | 2-3/day (7hr) |
| Kiel to Göteborg | Stena Line | daily (14hr) |

Denmark to Sweden

Dragør to Limhamn	Scandinavian	from 13
	Ferry Lines	daily (50min)
Tuborg to Landskrona	LT Line	3/day (1hr 20min)
Copenhagen to Malmö	Dampskibselskabet	hourly (40min)
	Öresund	
	MK Line (hovercraft)	10-11/day (35min)
Helsingør to Helsingborg	DSB/SJ	40/day (25min)
	·Scandinavian	every 15 min
	Ferry Lines	(25min)
Grenå to Helsingborg	Lion Ferry	2/day (4hr)
Grenå to Varberg	Lion Ferry	2-3/day (4hr)
Frederikshavn to	Stena Line	6/day (3^1/2hr)
Göteborg		

Sweden to Finland

Stockholm to Helsinki	Silja Line	daily (5hr)
	Viking Line	daily (15hr)
Stockholm to Mariehamn/	Silja Line	daily (13hr)
Turku	Viking Line	2/day (11hr)
Kapellskär to Nådendal/	Viking Line	2/day (9hr)
Naantali		
Sundsvall to Vaasa/Vasa	Vasabåtarna AB	from 6/week (9hr)
Umeå to Vaasa/Vasa	Vasabåtarna AB	from 1/day (4hr)

Island Ferries from Sweden

Bornholm (Denmark)

| Ystad to Rønne | Bornholmstrafikken | 2-5/day (2^1/2hr) |
| | (hovercraft) | |

Öland

| Oskarshamn to Byxelkrok | Ölandsund Line | 3/day (1hr 45min) |

Gotland

Oskarshamn to Visby	Gotlandsbolaget	daily (4^1/2hr)
Västervik to Visby	Gotlandsbolaget	daily (3^1/2hr)
Nynäshamn to Visby	Gotlandsbolaget	daily (5hr)

Åland/Ahvenanmaa (Finland)

Stockholm to Mariehamn	Ålandslinjen	6/week (6hr)
	Silja Line	daily (5hr)
	Viking Line	daily (5hr)
Kapellskär to Mariehamn	Viking Line	4/day (2^1/2hr)
Grisslehamn to Eckerö	Eckerö Line	5/day (2hr)

2. Advice to Car Drivers

In 1967 Sweden changed over from driving on the left to driving on the right. Though this has brought the country into line with the rest of continental Europe, it means that British visitors now face the same problems in adapting to driving on the right as elsewhere in Europe. But provided both driver and passengers are eternally vigilant on this matter, it should not pose any great problems. Headlamps should be fitted with special stick-on shades, normally issued by ferry companies with the tickets, so as to prevent them from dazzling other traffic. A nationality identity plate should also be attached to the rear of the vehicle.

Speed limits tend to be lower than in Britain for example, but are indicated by signs on all roads. The maximum speed in built-up areas is 50km/h (31mph). Otherwise the normal speed limit is 70km/h (43mph), but on good roads it is sometimes raised to 90km/h (56mph). Motorways and a few other long-distance routes have a speed limit of 110km/h (68mph). A car towing a caravan or trailer must not exceed 70km/h (43mph) on any road. A car towing a caravan without brakes must not go over 40km/h (25mph). Windscreen washers and wipers are compulsory, together with rear mudguards. Persons under 18 years old may not travel on motor bikes, whether as the driver or the passenger.

Where traffic priorities are not indicated, then traffic coming from the right always has priority. Trams have priority over all other vehicles. An unbroken white line in the middle of the road means that traffic may not cross this line to overtake unless there is a broken line inside it. Any yellow lines in the middle of the road are no longer valid. Overtaking is forbidden near all intersections.

Parking on the street may be restricted to certain times of day; these times are indicated by means of signs. If they are given in brackets, then the restriction applies only on Saturdays or on days before public holidays (see page 193). If they are in red, the restriction applies only on Sundays or public holidays.

Drivers are advised to beware of long vehicles carrying timber, which are liable to cut across the path of oncoming traffic on bends. This can be dangerous, especially in hilly or mountainous areas. All vehicles in Sweden must travel with dipped headlights at all times of the day or night. This regulation was introduced for the purposes of improving safety, especially in difficult terrain. The use of rear fog lamps is forbidden.

There are special regulations governing the use of diesel-powered vehicles. Dormobiles with a total weight of more than 3.5t and with seating for up to eight people (including the driver) are treated as heavy goods vehicles for the purposes of road tax. The same applies to vans weighing over 3.5t without seating for passengers. Dormobiles with seating for more than eight people including the driver are treated as buses for the purposes of road tax). In all such cases the driver must fill in a special road-tax form on entering the country, and must then pay the appropriate tax for the estimated distance to be travelled. When the vehicle is taken out of the country, the tax is adjusted to take account of the actual distance travelled.

No special documents are required for other vehicles, caravans, trailers or boats entering the country on a temporary basis for a period of less than 12 months. A current driving licence is of course necessary, and the green insurance card is recommended though not compulsory.

Petrol prices are not significantly different from those in Britain, and petrol grades are roughly equivalent. Most petrol stations close at six in the evening. Some of them have automatic pumps which will take 10skr notes and produce the appropriate amount of petrol. These are indicated by the sign *Lågpris*

The Swedish Touring Club office, Stockholm

Nattöppet-Automat. Drivers are recommended to fill up with petrol well in time, because petrol stations in Sweden are few and far between, and many are out of action over the weekend. A spare can of petrol is also recommended, with enough petrol for 50km.

Swedish traffic signs mostly follow the European standard, except that a white background is often replaced by yellow. Drivers who arrive in southern Sweden are often amused at the elk warning signs. These should, however, be taken seriously. The author once encountered an elk on the edge of Stockholm which forced him to break dangerously with a caravan on tow.

In all Scandinavian countries, it is forbidden for the driver of a foreign vehicle to allow a resident person to drive it, even on a temporary basis. If the vehicle is to be driven by any person other than the driver named on the car licence, then that person should have a written authorisation from the named driver.

Wearing of seat belts is compulsory in all vehicles which are fitted with them. For assistance in case of accident, there is an organisation called the KAK (*Kungliga Automobil Klubben* or 'Royal Automobile Club') (see page 235). Emergency telephones are located at infrequent intervals along the highways. The KAK can also be reached from public telephone boxes or private houses (which in Sweden almost always have telephones). It is entered in telephone directories under the term *Larmtjänst*. The

Grand Hotel, Stockholm

emergency telephone number (equivalent to 999 in Britain) in Sweden is 90 000. This can also be used to call the police, fire or ambulance services, or to reach the nearest doctor on duty outside normal working hours.

3. Accommodation in Sweden

Hotels and Guesthouses

The large hotels in cities such as Stockholm, Göteborg and Malmö are uniformly similar to international hotels elsewhere. But the same cannot be said of hotels and guesthouses in smaller towns or in the country, which vary enormously in their decor and layout, from the comfortably plush to the quaintly rustic.

In the big cities it is not always easy to find hotel accommodation, so it is worth making enquiries at the local tourist office. Similar information is also available in smaller towns. It is sensible to check the prices before committing oneself, so as to avoid any nasty surprises later on.

Hotels and guesthouses in Sweden are always kept spotlessly clean. But the shortage of menial staff means that luxury hotels

Chalets are popular for winter holidays

Camping by the lakeside

offer few of the extra services that might be expected elsewhere. Luggage must normally be taken up to the rooms by the guests themselves, and there is no one to clean the guests' shoes, except perhaps occasionally in Stockholm or Göteborg (automatic shoe-cleaners are provided instead). Breakfast is usually self-service, while room service is rare, and is enormously expensive in those few places where it is still available.

Chalet village, Småland

Holiday Cabins

This peculiarly Swedish kind of accommodation is plentiful in all
the main tourist areas. Holiday cabins come in a wide variety of
sizes and shapes, and they can be rented for any length of time
above a minimum of four nights. They are often in the form of the
traditional log cabin. They have good kitchen facilities and a
fireplace with a plentiful supply of logs. There is a wide choice of
sizes to suit different accommodation needs, from couples to
whole parties. They are often built together in large estates or
holiday villages, with a variety of facilities attached, such as
restaurants, sports centres and saunas. The sauna — in Swedish
bastu — is almost as typical of Sweden as it is of Finland.

Camping

Camping is very popular in Sweden, and the number of camping
sites has greatly increased in recent years. All the tourist areas
provide a wide range of excellent sites, with all facilities laid on.
This is particularly true of the many bathing resorts along the
coasts of southern Sweden. The big official sites often have a
swimming pool and other sports facilities attached. For those who
want to be 'closer to nature', there is a wide choice of more
primitive sites, often surrounded by the most glorious scenery.

Sites vary enormously in size, and often provide additional cabin accommodation, ranging from simple huts to fully-fledged holiday cabins (see above). Campers are often glad to be able to take their sleeping bags into one of these huts if the weather suddenly turns nasty or they are too tired to put up a tent.

The further north one goes, the fewer the official camping sites, but the more opportunities there are for 'free' camping on the edge of the forest or by the shores of a beautiful lake. Tents may be erected on any site in Sweden where it is not specifically forbidden, provided that it is at least 200m from the nearest house (see page 192) and not in a military zone. Those wishing to camp on recognisably private land should ask permission from the owner, which is normally generously given. Conversely, failure to ask such permission will generally result in being promptly ejected. It need hardly be repeated, in this most environmentally-minded of countries, that the site must never be damaged and the lighting of fires is strictly forbidden.

The Swedish tourist authorities offer a number of different hotel, camping and car-hire vouchers, which can be of great assistance when touring the country. Details of the options available can be obtained from the Swedish National Tourist Office (see page 233).

4. Food and Drink

As might be expected in a country as large as Sweden, there is a wide variety of specialities available, some of which are only to be found within certain areas.

In Sweden, as often in Britain, the rhythm of mealtimes has been adjusted to accommodate the fact that women go out to work as well as men. The Swedish breakfast is more modest than its Norwegian or Danish equivalent, and tends to be more like the so-called continental breakfast that is found elsewhere in Europe. The hotels usually provide a choice of different types of bread, including various sorts of crispbread. This is normally served with butter, jam and marmalade (and sometimes cheese as well), and with tea or coffee to drink. Breakfast is nearly always self-service. In country areas there is often a large jug of milk on the table, and country guesthouses often add a few specialities of their own. Special orders are often catered for, and the larger city hotels may even provide an English breakfast on request. For those who prefer to have breakfast outside their hotels (this is never frowned upon), there are plenty of snack bars in the cities providing good, cheap breakfasts.

Lunch at midday is usually no more than a snack. The only time a Swede will eat a full midday meal is when he is eating out with guests. The Swedes have their own equivalent of afternoon tea, except that coffee is the usual drink. It is normally accompanied by cake or biscuits. Like the British coffee and tea breaks, it is fully recognised by all Swedish employers. The main meal of the day is usually eaten between five and seven in the evening, when the family has come home from work. Every meal is followed by the obligatory cup of coffee — and that usually means two cups in Sweden. Sweden, like Germany, has made coffee its national drink, and the Swedes are among the world's biggest consumers of coffee. They normally drink it strong, though the beans are more lightly roasted than in Central European countries.

Swedish cuisine is associated in most people's minds with the *smörgåsbord* (cold table), with its wide selection of open sandwiches, beautifully prepared with all kinds of fish, meat and sausages. The emphasis is on fish, and especially on herring (in Swedish *sill*) — and fillet of autumn herring is a particular delicacy. Herring is often used as a starter instead of soup, which is rare in Swedish restaurants. It should not be imagined that the *smörgåsbord* is the usual main dish in Sweden. At home it is used purely on special occasions, and it is provided at only the most expensive of restaurants. This is simply because a proper *smörgåsbord* takes so long to prepare. The best place to sample it is at a specialist restaurant or on the ferry crossing to Sweden.

However, Swedish cuisine has a great deal more to offer than just *smörgåsbord* and herring — though herring itself comes in a vast number of delicious guises. One thing that always surprises foreign visitors to Sweden is the sweetness of many of their dishes. But for those who do not like this, a little lemon juice is all that is needed to transform them into something quite delicious. Sweden has no specifically national dishes. The coastal regions produce a variety of seafood dishes from the best that they have, while in inland areas the red trout is a particular speciality. As in other northern countries, salmon in all its forms — whether fresh or smoked, hot or cold — is a delicious if expensive delicacy. The crab feasts that take place in the late summer are an experience not to be missed, in which delicious crab dishes are accompanied by a large quantity of alcohol.

There are also some delicious meat dishes available, whether in the form of roasts, the popular *köttbullar* (meatballs) or sausages. They are usually served with potatoes rather than rice, and with vegetables when they are available. Salads are also popular, and are served with a piquant dressing. Unfortunately, the long Swedish winter means that fresh salads and vegetables are not always available, so that the Swedes themselves often have to supplement their diet with various vitamin preparations. Restaurants in the country, and especially in the north, offer a number of tasty reindeer dishes, often prepared and served in special pans and crockery.

The main course is always followed by a sweet of some sort. This will usually be some form of table cream or sweet soup, or maybe a pancake. Nowadays there is often a choice of a piece of cake or gateau, or even fresh fruit. The sweet is then followed by the standard cup of coffee. The Swedes usually drink milk or beer with their meals, or sometimes lemonade with their lunch. Swedish beer is very low in alcohol, and purists would call it no more than a 'beer-like drink'. The Swedes rarely drink ordinary water with their meals, reserving it purely for cleaning their teeth or for swallowing pills!

All restaurant meals in Sweden are expensive. As in Britain (and in contrast to countries such as Germany), restaurants are used primarily for eating rather than drinking. Self-service restaurants are common, and are usually more reasonably priced. It should be noted that *a bar* in Sweden is a snack bar, which sells no alcoholic drinks. A *kafé* is usually a small restaurant or snack bar, serving beer rather than coffee. The nearest equivalent to the British café or tea room is the *konditori*, in which coffee is usually accompanied by cakes. The restaurants are usually more interesting and friendly in the country than in the big cities. Nightclubs are virtually unknown in Sweden, since licensing laws apply right across the board.

Like other Northern Europeans, the Swedes like to drink plenty and often, and have a preference for spirits such as schnapps (in Swedish *snaps*). Alcoholism has become a serious problem in Sweden, and drastic measures have been taken to combat this. Until a few years ago, alcohol was strictly rationed in Sweden (as is still the case in Finland). Nowadays consumption is limited by means of exorbitantly high taxes. Spirits cost a good deal more than in Britain, and several times more than elsewhere in

Frösö golf course

continental Europe. And yet a small glass of *snaps* is still considered an essential aperitif for a really good meal. Imported drinks such as French, German and Portuguese wines are also heavily taxed, and are only drunk on very special occasions.

Beer is the most popular drink. Those who can afford it buy imported beers from Denmark, Germany or Czechoslovakia. Swedish beer, known as *öl*, comes in a number of different forms. The kind which is served at lunchtime or during the day is the lightest form, but resembles light ale in colour only. So-called *Pilsner* (which has nothing to do with Pilsen!) is also a light form, while *lageröl* or *mörköl* is darker but scarcely more substantial. The low-alcohol varieties (under 1.8 per cent) such as *lättöl* are available at ordinary food shops, whereas stronger beers such as *mellanöl* (3.6 per cent) are available only in certain restaurants, and then only after midday (one o'clock on Sundays). The alcohol content is always given on the label or container.

Strong or imported beers, together with wines and spirits, are only available at certain specially licensed stores, which belong to a state monopoly, and are not allowed to advertise. After dinner at home, the Swedes like to drink beer or *grogg* — a spirit mixed with lemonade or tonic. Then, later in the evening, they often have

Hunting in Lapland

a small supper snack consisting of a sandwich or two.

5. Sport in Sweden

Football is the Swedes' national sport, though it is played in summer rather than winter. Important matches attract vast audiences to the big city stadiums, which are provided with all modern facilities. The Swedish national football team is a force to be reckoned with in international tournaments.

Water sports are probably the other most popular summer activity. Middle-class Swedes very often have a small summer residence near to a lake, so it is not surprising that a very high proportion of them have their own yacht or motor boat. There are plenty of boat-hiring facilities available for visitors from abroad, both on the coast and by the many inland lakes. (For useful addresses, see page 231.)

Sweden offers a variety of facilities for other sporting activities, including tennis, golf and athletics. In the winter, ice hockey is as popular a spectator sport as football is in the summer, and Sweden has many teams of international

Fish are plentiful throughout Sweden

standard.

Not surprisingly, the most popular winter sporting activity is skiing. The climate is especially well-suited to cross-country skiing, while alpine skiing centres are mostly confined to more mountainous areas. They are equipped with all modern facilities, including ski-lifts, jumping slopes and tourist hotels, which provide countless opportunities for practice and enjoyment. In many areas skiing is possible well into the spring. The short days of the northern winter mean that expensive lighting is needed on many of the slopes and runs. The importance of skiing in Sweden is indicated by the large number of international stars that it has produced in proportion to its size.

Hunting in Sweden

The endless forests of central and northern Sweden make it a hunter's paradise that is rarely equalled elsewhere in Europe. Elk are found all over Sweden, and the annual elk hunts at the beginning of October attract thousands of game-hunters from far and wide. Southern Sweden also has a large population of red deer and smaller game such as pheasants and partridges. In northern Sweden these are further supplemented by ptarmigan, black grouse and capercaillie. Strict regulations prohibit the shooting of rarer species such as the brown bear, the glutton (the European equivalent of the wolverine), the Arctic fox and many birds of prey.

The tourist offices provide information on the means by which hunting licences are made available to visitors from abroad. The import of firearms is subject to the issue of a licence, for which proof is required that the visit is for the purposes of hunting. Special tours are organised for the elk hunt at the beginning of October, in which firearms licence, insurance and accommodation are included in the price. Details about these can be obtained from the Swedish National Tourist Office (see page 233).

Angling and Fishing

Sweden is also a paradise for anglers. For apart from 7,000km of coastline, there are also about 100,000 lakes. Salmon has become less plentiful in the rivers since the building of many hydroelectric power stations. However, several good salmon rivers remain, including the Mörrumså, the Ätra, the Dalälv (near Älvkarleby), the Kalixälv and the Torneälv.

Other species of the salmon and trout family are plentiful in rivers and lakes throughout Sweden. They are native to the more mountainous regions, while the populations elsewhere have been introduced. The lake fish also include pike, perch and similar species. The fish caught on the Baltic coast include cod and relatives of the salmon such as whitefish, grayling and sea trout. Those caught on the Skagerrak include cod, whiting, mackerel and sea trout. In the Sound it is sometimes even possible to catch tunny fish during their migrations through the strait.

The Swedes themselves are allowed to fish along most of their coasts without prior permission. But foreigners require a special permit, which can be obtained from the police and elsewhere. Certain parts of the coast are in military zones (see page 192) and are therefore prohibited to foreigners. Some rivers and lakes are under private ownership, and anglers must obtain permission from the landowner before fishing there. In most cases this involves the purchase of an angler's permit for a specified area and for a specific length of time. The prices of such angler's permits vary enormously, but they can be obtained from hotels, sports shops and tourist offices bearing the following symbol:

6. Tips for Travellers

Passports
British visitors entering Scandinavia require a valid passport but
no visa. US and other visitors are advised to check with the
consulate. Contrary to previous regulations, the head of a family
can now enter Scandinavia alone using a family passport in his
name.

Car Licence
A current licence is sufficient for temporary visitors up to a period
of twelve months. A nationality identity plate should also be
attached to the rear of the vehicle. Third-party insurance is
compulsory, but immediate proof of this is no longer required.

Car Hire
Sweden has a comprehensive network of local and international
car-hire firms. Some airline and ferry companies offer car-hire
facilities, and arrange for the car to be ready for collection on
arrival at the airport or ferry port. Some hotels also provide car-
hire facilities. In addition, car-hire vouchers can be obtained in
combination with hotel vouchers.

Customs Regulations
Customs are usually no problem when entering Sweden. A verbal
declaration is normally perfectly acceptable, and luggage is only
rarely searched. One is usually only questioned on entering
Scandinavia for the first time, and questions are normally about
alcohol and tobacco.
   Customs allow visitors to bring in a reasonable amount of
holiday equipment and personal effects. Boats and their
associated equipment may also be brought in without hindrance.
European visitors may each bring in a maximum of 200 cigarettes
or 100 cigarellos or 50 cigars and 250g of tobacco, a maximum of
one litre of spirits and one litre of wine per person, and 2 litres of
beer. Alcohol is forbidden to people under 20 years of age, and
tobacco to those under 15. Non-European residents may bring in
a maximum of 400 cigarettes or 200 cigarellos or 100 cigars or
500g of tobacco and the same quantity of other duty free items as
European residents. In addition, the import of fresh meat and
potatoes is banned. Other goods are allowed in up to a value of
600skr. Customs officers will be generous towards visitors with

camping equipment.

Firearms are subject to strict regulations, but permission can be obtained from the nearest consular authority. CB radios may only be used with the permission of the Swedish radio authority (address: Televerkets Radiodivision, Tillståndskontoret, S-12386). Further details about these regulations can be obtained from the Swedish National Tourist Office.

Quarantine Regulations

It is basically forbidden to bring live animals or plants into Sweden. This rule effectively applies to pets as well, although they can be imported under certain conditions. First a permit must be obtained from the Swedish consulate on submission of a medical certificate from an officially recognised body. Then the animals must be kept in quarantine on arrival for a period of 4 months. The costs of this must naturally be borne by the importer.

Telephoning

The first thing one notices on a Swedish telephone is that the **0** on the dial comes before the **1** instead of after the **9**. The international dialling code for Britain from Sweden is **009 44**, for the US, **009 1**. One should then wait for a tone before dialling the area code (minus the initial **0**), followed by the individual telephone number. For example, when ringing Leeds **(0532)** in England from Sweden, one dials **009 44**, followed (after the tone) by **532** and the number. International calls from a callbox run into the same problem as from a non-international callbox in Britain: the machine keeps swallowing up the coins, making communication very difficult.

A telephone call to another number on the same exchange costs 1skr, whatever the length of the call. The emergency number from anywhere in Sweden is **90 000**. When consulting a Swedish telephone directory, remember that the letters **å**, **ä** and **ö** (in that order) come at the end of the alphabet after **z**. The international dialling code for Sweden from Britain is **010 46**, from the US, **011 46.**

Post

Most post offices in Sweden are open on weekdays from 9am to 6pm, and on Saturdays from 10am to 12 noon or 1pm. Postage stamps are available from booksellers, stationers and newsagents as well as post offices. Postal rates (as of winter 1987) are as follows:

	Europe	**Elsewhere**
postcards and		
letters up to 20g	2.90skr	3.40skr
letters up to 50g	5.80skr	7.50skr

Currency and Exchange

The main unit of currency is the Swedish crown or krona, which is abbreviated to skr. In winter I987 there were approximately 10.38skr to the pound and 6.72skr to the dollar.

There are 100 öre to the krona. The coins are valued at 10 and 50 öre, 1skr and 5skr, the notes at 10skr, 50skr, 100skr, 500skr, 1,000skr and 10,000skr. Smaller coins from Denmark and Norway are normally not accepted in Sweden, because the Swedish krona has a higher value than the Norwegian or Danish krone. The import and export of Swedish currency is limited to 6,000skr, with no notes above 100skr. There are no such restrictions on importing foreign currency.

Medical Care

There is always medical treatment available, but because of the great distances in Sweden, this can often involve long journeys and waiting times. It is therefore important to take all the first aid and medicines one is likely to require, and maybe to seek the advice of one's own general practitioner beforehand. All medicines that go beyond the category of first aid require a doctor's prescription in Sweden.

The Swedes are extremely careful about hygiene. Medical treatment is free for all Swedish citizens, and is subsidised for foreigners, depending on reciprocal arrangements with the country concerned. British visitors are advised to apply to the Department of Health and Social Security well in advance, who will issue a leaflet giving details of reciprocal arrangements, plus an application form for a certificate of entitlement. Holiday insurance is also recommended.

Hospital treatment is free but out-patient treatment and medicine incurs a minimal charge of about 50skr, which must be paid in cash. The emergency telephone number is **90 000**, which can be used to call an ambulance or the nearest doctor on duty outside normal surgery hours.

US visitors are advised to contact their consulate to discover the arrangements open to them and should at least take out short-term full-cover medical insurance before leaving home.

Electricity
Electricity is Sweden's main form of energy, and is relatively cheap. On camping sites it is often provided free of charge, and most holiday cottages have electric heating. But before plugging anything in, it is vital to ask about the voltage. For although 220V AC is now standard, there are still some areas left which have direct current and voltages varying between 127V and 220V. Electrical devices such as shavers or hair-driers will be immediately ruined if plugged into direct current. Plugs and sockets have been standardised, but British plugs do not normally fit them. Hotels usually provide adaptors, but it is also possible to make one up for oneself by taking an extension lead and replacing the plug with a Swedish one.

Maps
A good map is essential for anyone who contemplates driving around Sweden. Good general maps are available to a scale of 1:1,000,000, but these lack detail, especially in the thinly populated areas in the north. So it is worth buying more detailed maps of the areas one proposes to visit, either at a specialist map shop or on arrival in Sweden. Also recommended is the *KAK-Bil kator* — the official road atlas of the KAK (see page 235), which can be ordered specially from booksellers.

Rights and Regulations
The Swedes are a very liberal-minded people, and respect one another's space. But in turn they expect others to respect their own space. Sweden is relatively free from prohibition signs and fences. The only common 'no entry' signs are those applying to motorised vehices. These are round signs with red letters in a red circle against a white or yellow background, and they usually say *'Ej obehöriga motorforden'* or *'Infart förbjuden'*. Such signs should always be taken seriously.

   The public are generally allowed access to private land, the only exceptions being private houses and their gardens, and parks where an entry fee is charged. This is all part and parcel of the Swedish principle of *allemannsrätten* (literally 'everyman's rights'), which grants public right of way to all land. Anyone is allowed to bathe in a lake or camp on open land without hindrance, provided that no damage occurs. If the land is clearly private, then permission should be sought from the owner, but it is almost always granted. The only restriction is the so-called *hemfridszone*, whereby rights are curtailed within 200m of the nearest building. Within this area, for example, the owner of the building has the sole right to pick mushrooms and berries.

The Swedes come down heavily on anyone who damages the environment by such activities as collecting birds' eggs or picking protected species of plants (a list of which can be obtained from tourist offices). The lighting of fires is strictly forbidden except on specially fire-proofed sites. It is not difficult to imagine the dangers of uncontrolled fires in the vast Swedish forests. Environmental regulations are strictly enforced, and serious violations can sometimes even result in prison.

Sweden pursues an international policy of strict neutrality, but goes to great lengths to secure both peace and neutrality by means of the most up-to-date weapons and defences. There are, for example, the so-called *skyddsområde* — military zones in which foreigners' movements are subject to severe restrictions. It is forbidden to leave the highway or take photographs, and unnecessary stops are also forbidden. Foreigners must be able to identify themselves and justify their actions at all times.

Shopping in Sweden
There are many interesting things to buy in Sweden, although the variations in the exchange rates mean that they can sometimes be expensive for visitors.

The different regions of Sweden all have their own distinctive handicrafts. These include a whole variety of hand-made materials and clothing. There is also a marvellous selection of traditional Swedish woodwork and silverwork, which again varies from area to area. Among the brightly painted wood carvings are the horses of Dalarna, which make wonderful souvenirs and are available in many different sizes. Swedish glass is still famous throughout the world. Visitors are often allowed into the factories to see how glass-blowing is done, and the finished products are on sale on the premises. The headquarters of the Swedish glass industry is at Växsjö in southern Småland, which also has a world-famous glass museum.

The best places for shopping are often the big hypermarkets on the edges of the big cities, which are often different from those in Britain in having a large number of specialist shops under the

Tax-free shopping at Arlanda Airport

same roof.There are about 6,000 shops in Sweden which have a sign outside saying (in English) *'tax-free for tourists'*. This means that foreign visitors can gain exemption from most of the VAT charged on the goods which are sold there. On presentation of a valid passport, the foreign purchaser is issued with a cheque amounting to roughly 14 per cent of the value of the goods bought (Swedish VAT being 19 per cent). This can be cashed on the way home, either on the ferry or at the port or airport, provided that the goods are unopened, and that no more than 7 days have elapsed since the purchase of the goods. Further details about this can be obtained from the Swedish National Tourist Office.

Credit Cards
Credit cards are more generally accepted in Sweden than in some other European countries (West Germany, for example). Euro-cheques are also accepted.

Public Holidays
Apart from Sundays, the following public holidays are observed in Sweden: New Year's Day, Epiphany (6 January), Good Friday,

Easter Monday, May Day (1 May), Ascension Day, Whit Monday, Midsummer Day, All Saints' Day (the Saturday between 31 October and 6 November), Christmas Day and Boxing Day.

School Holidays
Most Swedish schools have their summer holidays from the beginning of June to the end of August, apart from a few exceptional areas. The Christmas holidays start just before Christmas and go on for 3 weeks to about 10 January. The Easter holidays are short, being no more than 1 or 2 days either side of Easter. All schools have a week's holiday at various times in February for winter sports.

7. The Language

Swedish has about 9 million native speakers in Sweden and about 370,000 in Finland. Like English, it is one of the Germanic languages, which belong to the Indo-European family of languages.

Gothic was the first of the Germanic languages to be written down, and was the language of Bishop Wulfila's Bible translation, part of which — the so-called *Codex Argenteus* — is housed in Uppsala University Library. This valuable document goes back to the sixth century AD. However, the runic inscriptions from the same period, which have been found all over Scandinavia, were in a different language — that of the Vikings, from which the modern Scandinavian tongues are descended. These are generally known as the North Germanic languages. Gothic belonged to the now extinct East Germanic branch, while the West Germanic group includes English, Dutch and German.

The modern Scandinavian languages include Icelandic, Faroese, Norwegian, Danish and Swedish (Lapp and Finnish belong to a different language family). The most distinctive feature of the Scandinavian languages is the way the definite article ('the') is tagged on to the end of the noun. In Swedish, for example, *väg* = 'road', *vägen* = '**the** road', *vägar* = 'roads', *vägarna* = '**the** roads' (an example of a common noun); *tåg* = 'train' or 'trains', *tåget* = '**the** train' *tågen* = '**the** trains' (a neuter noun).

Danish and Norwegian are the closest languages to Swedish.

All three languages are simpler grammatically than Icelandic or German. Swedish, like Danish (and some forms of Norwegian) has reduced the three genders of masculine, feminine and neuter to two: common and neuter. Like Norwegian, Swedish has special tonal accents on words of more than one syllable. But unlike both Danish and Norwegian, it has kept a variety of vowels in its plural endings, such as in *skogar* (= 'forests') and *flickor* (= 'girls'). These last two factors make Swedish a very musical-sounding language.

Swedish is not difficult to learn. The grammar is relatively simple, and the spelling is more regular than that of English or French. English includes some common words of Scandinavian origin, which came in at the time of the Danish invasions. Swedish borrowed a large number of words from Low German during the Middle Ages, which may be familiar to speakers of German or Dutch. When using a Swedish dictionary, please note that the three letters, **å**, **ä** and **ö** (in that order) come at the end of the alphabet after **z**.

Visitors from English-speaking countries need not be afraid of communication problems. The majority of Swedes speak English, which is compulsory at all Swedish schools. It is useful to have a few words or short phrases in Swedish. But it is better to say one word only than to repeat something complicated, thus giving the impression of being able speak the language properly.

8. Useful Words and Phrases

Pronunciation

In Swedish: *ä* and *ö* are like *a* in 'rake' and *u* in 'urge' respectively; *æ*, *ø*, *a* and *y* are pronounced like *a* in 'cake', the *u* in 'urge', the *a* in 'awe' and the *u* in the French 'lune' respectively; *O* is sometimes pronounced *oo*, *u* is almost the same as *y*; *c* before *e*, *i* or *y* = *s*, otherwise *k*; *ch* before *e*, *i*, *y* ,*ä* and *ö* = *sh*; in 'och' (and) *ch* = *k*; *d* before *j* at the beginning of a syllable is mute; *f* at the end of a syllable is pronounced *v*; *g* before *ä*, *e*, *i*, *ö* and *y* and after *l* and *r* is pronounced like a consonontal *y*, as is *gj*, before *o* and *u*; *k* before the vowels, *y* and as in *kj* is almost like the English 'ch'. *lj* = consonontal *y*; *sj* = *sh*; *sk*, *skj* and *stj* before the vowels are like *sh*; *tj*; before the vowels is like *ch*.

English — Swedish
Hi! — Hej!
Welcome — Välkommen
Hello — God dag
Good morning — God morgon
Good evening — God afton
Good night — Got natt
Goodbye —Adjö
ej,icke — not
fullvuxnen — adult
barn — child
min — my
din, er — your
trans,hennes,dess — his, her, its
Have a good journey — God tur!
I am called... — Jag heter...
I come from... — Jag kommer från...
Great Britain — Storbritannien
England, Wales — England, Wales
Scotland, Ireland — Skottland, Irland
the United States — Förenta Staterna
How are you? — Hur står det till?
Very well, thank you — Tack, mycket bra
Please ... — Var så god...
yes, no — ja, nej
Do you speak English? — Talar ni engelska?
I don't understand — Jag förstår icke
I understand a little Swedish — Jag förstår lite grand svenska
I speak English — Jag taler engelska
I speak French and German — Jag taler franska och tyska
What did you say? — Hur sa?
Would you please... — Var så god...
...talk a little more slowly — ... och tala lite långsammare
... write that down — ... och skriv upp det
Many thanks — Tack så mycket
Not at all — Tack igen
I have to go now — Jag måste gå nu
What a shame! — Det var synd
What is the time? — Vad är klockan?
It is one o'clock — Klockan är ett
It is a quarter to two — Klockan är en kvart över två
... half past two — ... halv tre (lit. 'half three')

... a quarter past three — ... en kvart i tre
four, five, six, — fyra, fem, sex,
seven, eight, nine, — sju, åtta, nio,
ten, eleven, twelve — tio, elva, tolv
yesterday, today, tomorrow — i går, i dag, i morgon
in the morning (am) — på förmiddagen
in the afternoon (pm) — på eftermiddagen
Sunday, Monday, Tuesday — söndag, måndag, tisdag,
Wednesday, Thursday, — onsdag, torsdag,
Friday, Saturday — fredag, lördag
hotel, guest-house — hotell, pensionat
Do you have a room free? — Finns det något rum ledigt?
I am staying for one night — Jag stannar en natt
When is breakfast? — När börjar servera frukost?
Where is the dining room? — Var är matsalen?
What is the voltage here? — Vilken ström är det här?
Is camping allowed here? — Får man tälta här?
Is the water drinkable? — Kan man dricka vattnet här?
restaurant — restaurang, värdshus
breakfast, lunch — frukost, lunch
dinner, supper — middag, kvällsmat
coffee, tea — kaffe, te
milk, water — mjölk, vatten
bread, butter — bröd, smör
jam, marmalade — marmelad
honey — honung
sugar, salt — socker, salt
soup, broth — soppa, buljong
trout, salmon — forell, lax
cod, herring — torsk, sill
meatballs, sausages — köttbullar, korv
game — vilt og fågel
reindeer, chicken — ren, ungtupp
boiled egg, fried egg — kokta ägg, stekta ägg
scrambled egg — äggrörre
potatoes, rice — potatis, ris
peas, runner beans — ärter, haricovert
strawberries, raspberries — jordgubbar, hallon
cheese, ice-cream — ost, glass
lemonade, beer — läskedryck, öl
red wine, white wine — rödvin, vittvin
Cheers! Your health! — Skål!

Where is the food good and cheap? — Var kan man äta bra
och billigt?
Is this table reserved? — Är det här bordet upptaget?
May I have the menu?— Kan jag få matsedeln?
Is there a typical Swedish dish? — Finns det någon typisk
svensk rätt?
I would like fish, meat — Jag skulle vilja ha fisk, kött
May I have a cup of coffee? — Kan jag få en kopp kaffe?
May I have the bill? — Kan jag få notan?
Where are the toilets? — Var är toaletten?
gentlemen, ladies — herrar, damer
Where can I buy bread? — Var kan jag kjöper bröd?
Where can I get ... ? — Var kan jag få ... ?
I need shoes — Jag behöver skor
Do you have a jacket? — Har ni en jacka?
I don't like the colour — Jag tycker inte om färgen
Can you show me something else? — Kan ni visa mig något
annat?
I like this — Det tycker jag om
How much does it cost? — Vad kostar det?
That is expensive — Det är för dyrt
Can you give me change? — Kan ni växla?
Where can I get change? — Var kan jag växla pengar?
Where is the train for Stockholm? — Varifrån går tåget till
Stockholm?
When is the connection for Lund? — När kan jag resar
vidare till Lund?
Is there a restaurant car? — Finns det restaurangvagn?
No, only a buffet car — Nej, bara en kafévagn
Excuse me, ... — Ursäkta, ...
Is this seat taken? — Är den här platsen upptagen?
This is my seat — De här är min plats
Which is the pier for the ship — Vilken kaj ligger båten till
to Visby?   Visby?
When does the ferry depart? — När går färja?
Does this bus go to Skansen? — Går det buss till Skansen?
Where does the bus go from? — Varifrån avgår bussen?
How do we get to Gripsholm? — Hur kommer vi till Gripsholm?
Which is the best way to Vaxholm? — Vilken väg är bäst till
Vaxholm?
Is this the right way to Malmö? — Är det hä den riktiga vägen
till Malmö?

Is it far? — Är det långt?
How long does it take? — Hur lång tid tar det?
How many kilometres is it? — Hur månge kilometer år det?
Can you show me it on the map? — Kan ni visa mig det på kartan?
I'm afraid I'm a stranger here— Tyvärr är jag inte härifrån
Where is the nearest petrol station? — Var är närmaste
                                                          bensinstation?
 My car has broken down — Jag har motorstopp
Can you help me? — Kan ni hjälpa mig?
right, left, straight on — höger, vänstre, rakt fram

FURTHER INFORMATION

Museums and Art Galleries

Admission charges have not been included as they are subject to change. Opening times also vary so it is advisable to check with the local tourist information office before setting out.

Albert Engström's Studio and Museum
Grisslehamn
Near Norrtälje
☎ (0175) 30890
Oil paintings, graphics and collected items of Swedish artist and writer.
Open: 1 May-17 June and 1-16 September, weekends, 12noon-5pm; 18 June-31 August, daily, 12noon-5pm.

Archipelago Museum
Stavsnäs
Over 3,000 artifacts pertaining to the archipelago.
Open: June, August, Sundays, 12noon-3pm; July, weekends, 12noon-3pm.

Biological Museum
Djurgården
Stockholm
☎ (08) 611383
Flora and fauna of Sweden.
Open: April-September, daily, 10am-3pm.

Carl Eldh's Studio
Lögebodavägen 10
Bellevue Park
Stockholm
☎ (08) 306560
The sculptor's residence, now a museum to his life and work.
Open: May-September, Tuesday-Sunday, 12noon-4pm.

Cartoon Museum
Norrtälje
☎ (0176) 19833
Cartoons from 1890-1981.
Open: 15 May-14 September, Monday-Friday, 12noon-4pm, Saturday, 10am-2pm; 15 September-14 May, Wednesday-Friday, 12noon-4pm, Saturday, 10am-2pm.

City Museum
Peder Myndes backe 6
Stockholm
☎ (08) 440790
History and development of Stockholm.
Open: January-May, September-December, Monday, Friday, Saturday, Sunday, 11am-5pm; rest of week,11am-9pm; June-August, Monday, Friday, Saturday, Sunday,11am-5pm; rest of week, 11am-7pm.

Design Centre
Norrlandsgatan
Stockholm
☎ (08) 100377

Design exhibitions.
Open: 24 October-31 December,
Tuesday, Wednesday, 10am-5pm,
Thursday, 10am-7pm, Friday,
10am-5pm, Saturday, 12noon-4pm;
to 23 October, Tuesday-Saturday,
11am-5pm, Sunday, 12noon-4pm.

Far Eastern Museum
Skeppsholmen
Stockholm
☎ (08) 244200
Eastern art, handicrafts, porcelain,
Japanese watercolours, Indian
Buddhas, Stone Age Pottery.
Open: All year, Tuesday, 12noon-
9pm, Wednesday-Sunday, 12noon-
4pm.

Glass Museum
Södra Järnvägsgatan
Växjö
☎ (0470) 45145
Biggest museum of glassware in
northern Europe.
Open: Monday-Friday, 9am-4pm,
Saturday, 11am-3pm, Sunday, 1pm-
5pm.

Hallwyl Museum
Hamngatan 4
Stockholm
☎ (08) 102166
Housed in palace, displays the
collectables of Countess von
Hallwyl.
Open: January-April, Tuesday-
Sunday, 12noon-3pm; May-
August, Tuesday-Sunday, 11am-
2pm; September-December,
12noon-3pm.

Historical Museum
Narvavägen 13-17
Östermalm
Stockholm
☎ (08) 7839400

One of Stockholm's most
interesting museums: gold, silver,
treasures of the Vikings.
Open: All year, Tuesday-Sunday,
11am-4pm.

Hologram Gallery
Drottninggatan 100
Stockholm
☎ (08) 105465
3D pictures; remarkable portrait
collection.
Open: 1 January-10 May,
weekends,11am-4pm; 11 May-11
June, Tuesday, Wednesday,
12noon-5pm, Thursday,
Friday, 11am-5pm, weekends,
11am-4pm; 12 June-2 September,
Tuesday-Thursday, 11am-5pm,
weekends, 11am-4pm; 3 September -31 December, weekends,
11am-4pm.

**House of the East India
Company**
Norra Hamngatan 12
Göteborg
Historical, archaeological and
ethnographical collections.
Open: May-August, Monday-
Saturday, 12noon-4pm, Sunday,
11am-5pm; January-April,
September-December, Tuesday-
Saturday, 12noon-4pm,
Sunday, 11am-5pm.

Industrial Museum
Åvägen 24
Göteborg
The development of industry over
three centuries.
Open: May-August, Monday-
Saturday,12noon-4pm, Sunday,
11am-5pm; January-April,
September-December, Tuesday-
Saturday, 12noon-4pm, Sunday,
11am-5pm.

Liljevalch Art Gallery
Djurgårdsvägen 60
Stockholm
☎ (08) 144635
Contemporary art.
Open: All year, Tuesday,
Thursday, 11am-9pm, Wednesday,
Friday, weekends, 11am-5pm.

Limhamn's Museum
Limhamnsvägen 102
Malmö
☎ (040) 157810
Old Soldier's house fitted out as
fisherman's house.
Open: Wednesdays, 6pm-8pm,
weekends, 1pm-4pm.

Malmö Museum
Malmöhus Castle
Malmöhusvägen
Malmö
☎ (040) 73330
Art, archaeology, history.
Also on Malmöhusvägen are the
Technical Museum, Marittime
Museum, Carriage Museum and
Arsenal.
Open: Tuesday-Saturday,
12noon-4pm, Sundays, 10am-4pm.

Mediterranean Museum
Fredsgatan 2
Gustav Adolf's torg
Stockholm
☎ (08) 630770
World-famous Cyprus and Egyptian
collections.
Open: All year, Tuesday, 11am-
9pm, Wednesday-Sunday, 11am-
4pm.

Museum of Art
Götaplatsen
Göteborg
Works of Old Masters, French and
Scandinavian art, exhibitions in
adjoining art gallery.

Open: May-August, Monday-
Saturday, 12noon-4pm, Sunday,
11am-5pm; January-April,
September-December, Tuesday-
Saturday, 12noon-4pm, Sunday,
11am-5pm.

Museum of Dance
Laboratiegatan 10
Östermalm
Stockholm
☎ (08) 678512
Costumes, masks, decorations,
dances on TV monitors.
Open: All year, Tuesday-Sunday,
12noon-4pm.

Museum of Maritime History
Djurgårdsbrunnsvägen 24
Norra Djurgården
Stockholm
☎ (08) 223980
Unique collection of ship models.
Open: All year, daily, 10am-5pm.

Museum of Modern Art
Skeppsholmen
Stockholm
☎ (08) 244200
Twentieth-century art; Picasso,
Dali, Matisse, Warhol etc.
Open: All year, Tuesday-Friday,
11am-9pm, weekends, 11am-5pm.

**Museum of Science and
Technology**
Museivägen 7
Norra Djurgården
Stockholm
☎ (08) 631085
Special mining section, adjoining
building houses **TV Museum,
Electronics Museum,
Ethnographic Museum**.
Open: All year, Monday-Friday,
10am-4pm, weekends, 12noon
4pm.

Museum of Swedish Architecture

Skeppsholmen
☎ (08) 246300
Swedish architecture and town planning, sailing boat *Chapman* moored outside, used as youth hostel (closed winter).
Open: January-May, Monday-Friday, 9am-5pm; July-December, Monday-Friday, 9am-5pm.

Music Museum

Sybillegatan 2
Östermalm
Stockholm
☎ (08) 633939
Built about 1640, large collection of musical instruments.
Open: All year, Tuesday-Sunday, 11am-4pm.

National Museum

Södra Blasieholmshamnen
Stockholm
☎ (08) 244200
Built in 1866, largest collection in Sweden: applied art, furniture, tapestries, glass, porcelain, silver and paintings.
Open: All year, Tuesday, 10am-9pm, Wednesday-Sunday, 10am-4pm.

Natural History Museum

Slottsskogen
Göteborg
Mammals, birds etc.
Open: May-August, Monday-Saturday, 12noon-4pm, Sunday, 11am-5pm; January-April, September-December, Tuesday-Saturday, 12noon-4pm, Sunday, 11am-5pm.

Natural History Museum

Brunnsviken
Stockholm
☎ (08) 150240
14 million plant and animal exhibits.
Open: All year, Monday-Saturday, 10am-4pm, Sunday, 11am-5pm.

Nordic Museum

Djurgården
Stockholm
☎ (08) 224120
Founded 1873, account of early Scandinavian peoples.
Open: June-August, Monday-Friday, 10am-4pm, weekends, 12noon-5pm; September-May, Tuesday, Wednesday, Friday, 10am-4pm, Thursday, 10am-8pm, weekends, 12noon-5pm.

Postal Museum

Nygatan 6
Stockholm
☎ (08) 7811755
Magnificent stamp collection.
Open: All year, daily, 12noon-3pm.

Röhsska Museum of Applied Art

Vasagatan 37-39
Göteborg
Furniture, textiles and glass.
Open: May-August, Monday-Saturday, 12noon-4pm, Sunday, 11am-5pm; January-April and September-December, Tuesday-Saturday, 12noon-4pm, Sunday, 11am-5pm.

Roslagen Museum

Norrtälje
☎ (0176) 11630
Displays artifacts of Norrtälje.
Open: 15 May-14 September, Monday-Friday, 12noon-4pm, Saturday,10am-2pm; 15 September - 14 May, Wednesday-Friday,12noon-4pm,Saturday 10am-2pm.

Royal Army Museum

Riddargatan 13
Östermalm
Stockholm
☎ (08) 603853/617602
Uniforms, medals, weapons, flags
of Swedish Army.
Open: All year, Monday-Saturday,
11am-4pm.

SJ Railway Museum

Rälsgatan 1
s-80108 Gävle
☎ (026) 129880
More than 40 locomotives and
railcars.
Open: 1 June-31 August, daily,
10am-4pm; 1 September-31 May,
contact museum for information.

Skansen

Djurgården
Stockholm
☎ (08) 670020/630500
Open-air museum, established
1891, contains more than 150 old
buildings, many of them occupied.
See traditional handicrafts.
Open: January-March, daily, 8am-
6pm, April, daily, 8am-8pm; May-
August, daily 8am-11.30pm,
September, daily, 8am-8pm;
October-December, daily, 8am-
6pm.

SL Transport Museum

Odenplan Subway Station
Stockholm
☎ (08) 236500/1351
Authentic horse tram, bus from
1928 etc.
Open: January-April, October-
December, Monday-Saturday,
10am-5pm.

Strindberg Museum

Drottninggatan 85
Stockholm
☎ (08) 113789
Last residence of dramatist August
Strindberg, from 1908-12.
Open: All year, Tuesday-Saturday,
10am-4pm, Sunday, 12noon-5pm.

Thiel Gallery

Blockhusudden
Djurgården
Stockholm
☎ (08) 625884
Large art collection.
Open: All year, Monday-Friday,
12noon-4pm, Sunday, 1pm-4pm.

Torekäll Mountain Park Museum

Old Södertälje
☎ (0755) 21000
Rural life and culture.
Open: All year, daily, 11am-4pm.

Toy Museum

Mariatorget 1
Södermalm
Stockholm
☎ (08) 416100/404492
One of the largest toy collections in
the world; over 10,000 exhibits.
Open: All year, Tuesday-Friday,
10am-4pm, weekends, 12noon-
4pm.

Wasa Museum

Djurgården
Stockholm
☎ (08) 223980
Mighty warship *Wasa*, 62m long
raised from harbour. Built 1625-8.
Open: January-1 June, Monday-
Sunday, 10am-5pm; 10 June-19
August, daily, 9.30am-7pm; 20
August-December, daily, 10am-
5pm.

Wine and Distillery Museum
St Eriksgatan 119
Stockholm
☎ (08) 333255
How to press, bottle and distil wine.
Mechanical 'sniffing' cabinet helps
you to distinguish between
Schnapps brands.
Open: All year, Tuesday-Friday,
10am-3pm.

Other Museums, Well Worth Visiting, May be Found at:

Älvdalen
Rotskans Estate: an open-air
museum.

Arjeplog
Museum Arjeplog: old Lapp
silverwork.

Arvidsjaur
Open-air museum.

Eskilstuna
Open-air museum.

Falun
Stora Kopparbergs Museum: old
copper workings and collection of
copper coins.

Gävle
Gamle Gävle: open-air museum.

Göteborg
Kronhuset; Kronhusgatan 1: the
history of Göteborg.
Military Museum, Skansen Kronan:
weapons and uniforms.
Museum of Medical History.
Museum of Theatre History,
Berzeligatan 1: the history of the
theatre in Göteborg from 1780 to
present.
School Museum, Engelbrektsgtn. 1

history of education.
Ship Museum, Lilla Brommen: open-
air museum.
Shipping Museum, Stigbergstorget:
the history of seafaring,
shipbuilding and fisheries.

Halmstad
Hallandsgård Museum.
Miniland: miniature town.

Jokkmokk
Lapp Museum: Lapp culture.

Jönköping
Match Museum: history of the
match industry.

Karlskrona
Shipping Museum: history of
shipping.

Linköping
Gamla Linköping: open-air museum
with old buildings from the
eighteenth and nineteenth
centuries.

Luleå
Museum of Lapp Art and Culture.

Lund
Art Museum: sketches, miniatures,
models.
Museum of Classical Antiquities:
ceramics, sculptures, coins.
Open-air Museum: farm buildings
and manor houses.
Zoological Museum: the fauna of
the area.

Malmberget
Mining Museum.

Malmö
Art Gallery, Magistratsparken.
Dolls Museum, Gustav Adolf's torg.
Sports Museum, Baltiska hallen.

Mariefred
Railway Museum.

Mora
Open-air Museum.
Zorngården: where famous artist,
Andreas Zorn lived.

Norrköping
Museum of Art.
Museum of Local History.

Östersund
Jamtli: Open-air Museum: one of
the largest in Sweden.

Umeå
Gammlia Open-air Museum:
historical buildings and museum of
Lapp culture.

Varberg
Varberg Museum: life of Halland
county.

Visby
Museum of Antiquities.

Churches and Cathedrals

Alskog
Eleventh-century church; nearby
are Bronze Age monuments in the
form of ships.

Alvastra
Ruined twelfth-century Cistercian
monastery.

Älvdalen
Beautiful fifteenth-century church.

Arboga
Twelfth-century stone church.

Barlingho
Thirteenth-century church with
twelfth-century font.

Dalby
Oldest surviving church in Sweden,
built 1060.

Falsterbo
Interesting fourteenth-century
church at this seaside resort.

Fide
Thirteenth-century church.

Gammelstad
Fifteenth-century church with
Flemish altar.

Göta Canal
Vreta Abbey on the south bank is a
twelfth-century church which
belonged to a Cistercian convent.

Göteborg
Göteborg Cathedral, completed
1825.
Örgryte Old Church, oldest building
in Göteborg, parts dating back to
thirteenth century.

Hackås
Church, parts of which go back to
the eleventh century; Romanesque
frescos.

Hagby
Twelfth-century Romanesque
round church.

Jokkmokk
Sixteenth-century Lapp church,
made of wood.

Kalmar
Seventeenth-century cathedral.

Karlskoga
Church with murals and ceiling paintings from 1723.

Kristianstad
Trinity Church, Danish Renaissance style.

Kungälv
Baroque church, built 1679

Leksand
Twelfth-century church, famous for midsummer celebrations.

Linköping
Fifteenth-century cathedral retains its Romanesque north doorway. Tower added in 1886.

Lund
Romanesque cathedral, consecrated 1145 – the finest in Europe; carvings, fourteenth-century astronomical clock.

Malmö
St Peter's Church, a fourteenth-century brick building, the second largest in Sweden, with Gothic frescos and Baroque altar.

Mora
Fourteenth-century church with separate bell tower.

Nättraby
Twelfth-century church.

Nordmaling
Fourteenth-century church.

Öja
Thirteenth-century church with beautiful Burgundian crucifix.

Pukavik
Twelfth-century church with lovely medieval frescos.

Rättvik
Church built in 1200, lovely frescos.

Roma
Twelfth-century church and ruins of Cistercian monastery, built 1164.

Särna
Wooden church, built 1244, heavily restored in the eighteenth century.

Sigtuna
Ruins of tenth and eleventh-century churches of St Olof, St Per and St Lars. Thirteenth-century St Mary's Church, pure Gothic in style.

Simrishamn
Twelfth-century church.

Söder Råda
Church with frescos, built 1350.

Sollentuna
Twelfth-century church.

Stockholm
Stockholm Cathedral, the oldest building in the city, founded 1260. Monarchs of Sweden crowned here.
German Church – late Gothic, founded in the sixteenth century by Hanseatic merchants.
Riddarholmen Church – burial place of Swedish monarchs and famous citizens.
Adolf Fredrik's Church, built 1774 in Baroque style.

St Clare's Church, built in 1753 in Gustavian style, contains museum of liturgical objects.
St James's Church, built 1643, tower 1735.

Stora Tuna
Fifteenth-century church with Gothic exterior and Baroque interior.

Strängnäs
Thirteenth-century cathedral.

Tierp
Fascinating fourteenth-century church, lovely frescos and thirteenth-century belltower.

Uppsala
Uppsala Cathedral, one of the largest in Scandinavia, Gothic in style, built twelfth century.
Trinity Church, parts are twelfth century, medieval wall paintings.

Vadstena
Convent, founded in the thirteenth century by St Birgitta.

Västervik
Beautiful fifteenth-century church of St Gertrude.

Ysane
Twelfth-century church with medieval wall paintings.

Ystad
St Mary's Church, built thirteenth century, tower added later.
St Peter's Church, built at the same time.

Buildings, Monuments and Other Places of Interest

Bergius Botanical Gardens
Brunnsviken
Stockholm
☎ (08) 153912
Largest water lily in the world – 7ft in diameter!
Open: March-October, daily ,1pm-4pm; November-February, daily, 1pm-3pm; June-September, Victoria House only, daily, 1pm-4pm.

Birka
Björkö
Ekerö Municipality
☎ (08) 241100
Oldest known city in Sweden, reached its zenith AD800-975.
Open: 5 May-3 June, weekends, 10am-5.30pm; 9 June-19 August, Tuesday, Wednesday, Thursday, weekends, 10am-5.30pm; 25 August-2 September,weekends, 10am-5.30pm.

Ceramics Centre
Gustavsberg
☎ (0760) 39100
Factory shop, porcelain painting, café.
Open: 14 May-8 September, Monday-Friday, 10am-3pm, Saturday, 10am-2pm.

City Hall Tower
Hantverkargatan 1
Stockholm
☎ (08) 7859000
View from tower over Stockholm is magnificent.
Open: May-September, daily, 10am-3pm.

Drottningholm Palace
Stockholm
☎ (08) 7590310
Seventeenth-century Renaissance
building, permanent home of royal
family. 608 rooms, antiquities.
Open: May-August, Monday-
Saturday, 11am-4.30pm, Sunday,
12noon-4.30pm; September, daily,
1pm-3.30pm.

Drottningholm Court Theatre
Drottningholm
Stockholm
☎ (08) 7590406
Unique theatre from the eighteenth
century. Original stage designs.
Open: 2 May-31 October, Monday-
Friday, 12noon-4.30pm; Sunday,
1pm-4.30pm; 1-30 September,
daily, 1pm-3pm.

Elfsborg Fortress
Göteborg
Seventeenth-century fortress built
to protect the city.
Open: 17 May-31 August, daily,
9.45am-5.30pm.

Fort Apache
Ytter-Enhörna Church
Near Enhörna
☎ (0755) 44209
Recreated Wild West town.
Open: 30 April-17 June and 21-29
August, weekends, 11am-6pm; 22
June -12 August, daily,11am-6pm.

Gripsholm Castle
Mariefred
☎ (0159) 10194
Finest and most interesting
Renaissance castle in Sweden.
Immense portrait collection,
furniture, original decor.
Open: 15 May-31 August, daily,
10am-4pm.

Gröna Lunds Tivoli
Djurgården
Stockholm
☎ (08) 603000
Pleasure park, circus, fair,
restaurants etc.
Open: 21 April-9 June and
20 August-9 September, Tuesday-
Friday, 7pm-midnight, Saturday,
2pm-midnight, Sunday, 12noon-
midnight; Saturday, 2pm-midnight,
Sunday, 12noon-10pm.

House of Culture
Sergel's Torg
Stockholm
☎ (08) 141120
Music, theatre, exhibitions,
debates etc.
Open: All year, Monday,
Wednesday, Thursday, Friday,
11am-6pm, Tuesday,11am-10pm,
weekends, 11am-5pm.

House of Nobles
Stockholm
☎ (08) 100857
Built seventeenth century in Dutch
Baroque style.
Open: All year, daily, 11.30am-
12.30pm.

House of Parliament
Riksgatan 3A
Helgeandsholmen
Stockholm
☎ (08) 7864000
Built 1893. Guided tours only.
Open: 1 July-13 September,
Monday-Friday, 12noon-3.30pm,
Saturday, 12noon-2pm; 1 October-
15 June, weekends, 12noon-2pm.

Kaknäs Tower
Norra Djurgården
Stockholm
☎ (08) 678030

155m high television tower, tallest
building in Scandinavia, marvellous
views.
Open: October-March, daily,
9am-6pm; April and September,
daily, 9am-10pm; May-August,
daily, 9am-midnight.

Millesgården

Carl Milles väg 2
Lidingö
Stockholm
☎ (08) 7650553
Sculptor's one-time residence.
Open: May-15 October, daily,
10am-5pm.

Museum Ships

Galävarvet
Djurgården
Stockholm
☎ (08) 223980
Ships *Finngrundet, Sankt Erik*
moored next to *Wasa* Museum.
Lightship and icebreaker from early
twentieth century.
Open: 9 June-18 August, daily,
12noon-5pm; 19 August-31
December, Sunday, 11am-4pm.

Örebro Castle

Svartån
Örebro
☎ (019) 130760
Open: Guided tours mid-June to
mid-August, 11am, 12noon, 1pm
and 3pm daily.

Pavilion of Gustav III

Haga Park
Stockholm
☎ (08) 7898500
Delightful interiors.
Open: May-August, Tuesday-
Sunday, 11am-3pm; September,
weekends,1pm-3pm.

Riddarhuset (Knight's House)

Riddarhustorget 10
☎ (08) 100857
Seventeenth-century, Dutch
Baroque style. 2,325 weapons.
Open: All year, Monday-Friday,
11.30am-12.30pm. Guided tours
only.

Riksdag Building

Riksgatan 3A
Stockholm
☎ (08) 7864000
Newly-refurbished seat of Riksdag,
Sweden's national legislature.
Erected 1905.
Open: 30 June-29 August, Monday-
Friday, 8.30am-11.30am.

Rosendal Palace

Djurgården
Stockholm
☎ (08) 118561
Built 1823-7 by King Karl XIV
Johan.
Open: June-August, Tuesday-
Sunday,12noon-3pm; September,
weekends, 1pm-3pm.

Rosersberg Palace

Rosersberg
☎ (0760) 35039
Built around 1800, interiors from
Charles XIII and Charles John XIV.
Open: 15 May-June and August,
Wednesday, Thursday, 10am-3pm,
Sunday, 12noon-3pm.

Royal Palace

Visningsvåningarna
Slottsbacken
Stockholm
☎ (08) 7898500
Three floors with stately
apartments: Treasury, Armoury,
Hall of State, Church, Museum,

Changing of the Guard. NB: All or parts of the palace may be closed without warning.
Open: for changing of the guard: January-May, Wednesday and Saturday at 12.10pm and Sunday at 1.10pm; June-August, Monday-Friday at 12.10pm, Saturday, 10am-2pm, Sunday at 1.10pm; September-December, Wednesday at 12.10pm, Sunday at 1.10pm.

Skokloster Castle
Near Sigtuna
☎ (018) 386077
Field Marshal Carl Gustav Wrangel's tremendous Baroque castle.
Open: May-September, daily,12noon-4pm.

Stockholm City Hall
Hantverkargatan 1
Stockholm
☎ (08) 7859000
Begun 1911, Golden Hall, Council Room, Blue Hall.
Open: All year, guided tours, Monday-Saturday, 10am, Sundays, 10am-12noon.

Svindersvik Manor
Nacka
Stockholm
☎ (08) 224120
Summer house from eighteenth century.
Open: 15 May-15 September, Sundays, 1pm-4pm.

Tullgarn Palace
On E4, near Vagnhärad
☎ (0755) 72011
Dates back to 1720s.
Open: 15 May-15 September, daily, 11am-4pm.

Tyresö Castle
Tyresö
Stockholm
☎ (08) 224120
Built 1620 by Count Gabriel Oxenstierna.
Open: 15 May-15 September, weekends, 12noon-4pm.

Vaxholm Fortress
Vaxholm
☎ (0764) 30100/387
Once protector of Stockholm, weapons, uniforms etc.
Open: 15 May-31 August, daily, 12noon-4pm. Boat runs half-hourly from Stockholm.

Vira Iron Works
Roslags-kulla
Near Stockholm
☎ (0764) 53180/53149
Founded 1630. Museum, coffee shop, exhibition, wrought iron handicrafts.
Open: 1 May-midsummer and 20 August-30 September, weekends, 11am-4pm; 25 June-19 August, daily,11am-4pm.

Waldemarsudde House
Prins Eugensväg 6
Djurgården
Stockholm
☎ (08) 621833
Art nouveau-style villa.
Open: January-May and September-December, Tuesday-Sunday, 11am-4pm, June-August, Tuesday-Sunday 11am-5pm.

Other Places of Interest May be Found at:

Åby
Kolmården Safari Park: largest of its kind in Europe.

Bohus
Bohus Castle: built 1310.

Borrby
Glimmingehus Castle: fifteenth
century, now used as a restaurant.

Eskilstuna
Eskilstuna Zoo: largest in Sweden.

Falun
Heden Castle.

Göteborg
Carolus Tower, Kungsgatan.
Skansen Kronan Tower: now a
museum.

Halmstad
Halmstad Castle: sixteenth to
seventeenth century.

Helgasjön, near Växjö
Kronoberg Castle: interesting
ruins.

Helsingborg
The Kärnan: tenth-century tower.
Kronenborg Castle.

Kållandsö
Läckö Castle.

Kalmar
Kalmar Castle: massive five-
towered structure, mostly
sixteenth to seventeenth century.

Katrineholm (3km west)
Prehistoric Settlement: the oldest
to have been discovered in
Sweden. Stone Age dwellings
5,000 years old.

Kivik
Kivik Monument: reconstruction of
Bronze Age tomb.

Kristianstad
Garvaregården, Tivoligatan:
seventeenth-century tanner's
workshop, now a restaurant.
Lillöhus Castle: fifteenth-century
ruins.

Landskrona
Sixteenth-century citadel.

Lurö
Ruined abbey.

Malmö
Malmöhus Castle: fifteenth
century, now museum of history of
Malmö and province of Skåne.

Mariestad
Mariestad Castle: built 1660, seat
of local government.

Norrköping
Himmelstalund Park: Bronze Age
rock drawings.
Ringstad Estate (6km N.W. of
Norrköping): remains of seventh-
century fortifications and
extensive burial site.

Nyköping
Nyköpingshus Castle.

Sala
Sala Silver Mines.

Stockholm
Birger Jarl's Tower: fifteenth-
century, fine views.
Crown Prince's Palace: built 1783,
houses foreign ministry.
Kungsträdgården: gardens
containing statue of Carl XIII and
monument to Carl XII. Open-air
theatre.
Royal Drama Theatre.
Royal Library.

Royal Opera House.
Stenbock Palace.
Wrangel Palace: mid-seventeenth century, houses Stockholm Supreme Court.

Sunne
Mårbacka: family estate of novelist Selma Lagerlöf.
Rottneros Manor: Neo-classical, 100 sculptures.

Svärtinge
Viking Fort: remains of seventh-century fort and burial site.

Uppsala
Uppsala University: oldest in Sweden.
Gunilla Bell: famous bell in wooden tower.

Vadstena
Vadstena Castle: Renaissance style.

Varberg
Varberg Fortress: thirteenth century, now a museum.

Värnarmo
High Chaparral: American Wild West mock-up.

Västerås
Engsö Manor: with Ängsö treasure.
Tidö Castle: contains toy museum.

Växjö
Bergkjara Castle: ruins from Middle Ages.

National Parks

Ängsö, Uppland

Blå Jungfrun, Småland

Abisko, Lapland

Dalby Söderskog, Skåne

Garphytten, Närke

Gotska Sandön, Gotland

Hamra, Dalarna

Muddus, Lapland

Norrakvill, Småland

Padjelanta, Lapland

Peljekaise, Lapland

Sarek, Lapland

Sonfjället, Härjedalen

Stora Sjöfallet, Lapland

Töfsingdalen, Härjedalen

Vadvetjåkko, Lapland

Winter Sport Resorts

These resorts cater for most winter sports. There is skiing in Sweden usually from November to mid-May. There is ample skiing all over the country from Småland in the south to Lapland in the north.

Abisko, Björkliden, Riksgränsen, Borgafjäll, Saxnäs
Dundred
Gäddede, Stora Blåsjön
Härjedalen with *Vemdalsfjäll, Funäsdalen, Bruksvallarna, Tänndalen, Tännäs* and

Fjällnäs
Idre and *Grövelsjon*
Isaberg
Jokkmokk
Lake Siljan with *Leksand, Rättvik*
and *Tällberg.*
Närke
Sälen
Storuman
Strömsund
Sunna
Sylarna, Storulvån, Blåhammaren,
Åre, Duved, Trille Vallen
Västmanland
Vilhelmina

Geographical Terms

å – small river
älv – river
ås - hillridge
berg – hill, mountain
bro – bridge
bukt – bay
dal – valley
färja – ferry
fjäll – mountain, fell
fors – waterfall
gata – street
glaciär – glacier
hav – sea
hed – heathland
höjd – peak
järnväg – railway
kärr, träsk – bog, marsh
klev – rock face
klint – cliff
köping – market town
kulle, klätt – low hill
kyrka – church
lid – slope of hill
mo, myr – moorland
ö – island
plats, plan – square
sjö – lake

skog – wood, forest
skola – school
slott – castle
stad – town
strand – beach, flat coast
ström – fast-flowing river, rapids
sund – arm of sea, strait
tjåkko – sharp peak
torg – market square
torn – tower
trädgård – garden, park
väg – road, way
vatten – water, lake
vik – inlet, gulf

Annual Events

January
Malmö
Boat Show

February
Arjeplog
Lapp Market
Gävle
International Motorcycle Ice Race
Jokkmokk
Lapp Winter Fair of Handicrafts

March
Dalarna
Vasa Run (cross-country ski-race)
Gällivare
Lapp Market with ski contests
Malmö
Malmex stamp exhibition
Stockholm
Antiques Fair
The Spring Salon: Art Show at
Liljevalch Exhibition Hall

April
Helsingborg
Frimynt (coin and stamp exhibition)
Jönköping
Gunnar Nilsson Show (sports and

race cars)
Stockholm
The Spring Salon: Art Show
Throughout Sweden
30 April Walpurgis Night

May
Älvkarleby
Waterfall Day
Jönköping
Scandinavian Game Fair
Råshult
Linnaeus Day
Stockholm
Kite Festival at Gårdet
Performances (opera etc) at
Drottningholm Court Theatre.
The world's longest Smörgåsbord,
Kungsgatan (not every year)
'Dagbladsstafetten,'– relay race for
elite and 'jogger' class runners

June
Anderstorp
Swedish Grand Prix (Formula 1)
Grisslehamn
Mail Rowing Race
Östersund
Expo Norr trade fair
Stockholm
Performances at Drottningholm
Court Theatre, Ulriksdal Palace and
in the parks of Stockholm
'Skärgardsbåtens Dag' –
Archipelago Boat Day
Stockholm Marathon
Jazz and Blues All-Star Festival,
Skeppsholmen
'The Nordic Music Festival'
Throughout Sweden
6 June Flag Day, 22-24 June,
Midsummer Festival

July
Halmstad
Salmon Festival
Helsingborg

Antiques Fair
Lycksele
Lapland Week
Ronneby
Tosia Bonnada'n (Folk Festival)
Sigtuna
Sigtuna Fair
Söderhamn
Herring Festival
Stockholm
'Bellman Week' (Bellman's Day is
26 July)
'Gotlands Runt' – yacht race
DN Gala – international track and
field meet

August
Stockholm
Swedish-American's Day,
festivities at Skansen
'Midnattsloppet'— the Midnight Run
St Erik's Fair
Strängnäs
European Motorboat
Championships, Lake Mälar

September
Stockholm
'Sailboat Day'
'Everything for the sea'— floating
boat show at Galärvarvet

October
Stockholm
'Lidingöloppet' – cross-country
race for elite and jogging class
runners
'Birgitta Day'

November
Stockholm
Dog Show, Fairground , Stockholm
Open Grand Prix Tournament
Throughout Skåne
Mårten Gås (St Martin's Day)

December
Stockholm
Nobel Day with presentation of the
year's prizes in economics,
medicine, physiology, physics and
chemistry
Coronation of Sweden's 'Lucia' for
the year at Skansen
Christmas markets and fairs
everywhere

Travelling to Sweden

By Sea
For details of ferry routes and
times, see pages 173-4. For more
detailed information contact the
ferry companies direct or the
Swedish National Tourist Office.

By Air
See page 169. Travellers are
advised to contact the airlines
direct for detailed times and prices.

By Coach
See page 168. Travellers are
advised to contact the bus and
coach travel companies or travel
agents for precise details.

By Rail
See page 198. Visitors to Sweden
should contact the Norwegian or
Swedish State Railways Travel
Bureau.

Travelling in Sweden

By Boat
The Swedish coastline is dotted
with thousands of islands, many of
which are linked to the mainland by
regular boat services. Steamer
trips can also be taken on many of

the larger inland waterways and
lakes. Some of the busiest
services link the Baltic island of
Gotland with the mainland.
Frequent car ferries operate to the
island's main harbour.

A classic tourist route is the Göta
Canal which links the great lakes
and archipelagos of central
Sweden with regular passenger
sailings between mid-May and early
September. Visitors to Stockholm
can buy a season ticket which
gives unlimited travel on the white
Stockholm archipelago boats for a
14-day period. You can hire boats
and motor cruisers in more than 30
places in Sweden or you can bring
your own boat with you on a trailer.
For details of island ferries from
Sweden, see page 174. Also,
contact the Swedish National
Tourist Office.

By Air
Air travel within Sweden is
remarkably inexpensive. SAS and
its associate airline LIN offer round-
trip 'mini-fares' every day on
selected flights and during the
peak tourist season (end June to
mid-August) cheap fares are valid
on all flights. The mini-fares
scheme offers round-trip travel for
the price of a one-way fare. For
more information, see page 171.
For detailed information on cheap
fares and routes, contact the
airlines or the Swedish National
Tourist Office.

By Coach
Coach services in Sweden provide
an inexpensive and comfortable
way of getting around the country,
offering fast connections between
Stockholm and the coastal towns in

the north. GDG operates daily express services from Göteborg to various parts of Sweden while Swedish State Railways (SJ) and several private companies operate weekend coach services to about 100 places. For additional information, see page 169. For more detailed information, contact the Swedish National Tourist Office.

By Rail

See page 169. Swedish State Railways provides a highly efficient network of services covering the whole of the country. On virtually all long-distance trains there is a restaurant car or buffet for meals, drinks and snacks. Swedish trains operate at a high frequency particularly along the main trunk routes linking Stockholm with Göteborg and Malmö. On some long distance trains special compartments marked 'BK' are available for nursing mothers. On some trains marked 'R' on the timetable it is necessary to make a reservation.

For details of special reduced fares, go-as-you-please tickets and rail passes contact the Swedish National Tourist Office, the Swedish or Norwegian State Railways Travel Bureau or your travel agent.

By Bicycle

Sweden's uncrowded roads are ideal for a cycle holiday. Cycle lanes are frequently provided in cities and cycles can be hired easily – just ask at the local tourist office. The Swedish Touring Club (STF) in Stockholm provides information on cycling

packages.

Public Transport

In the major towns it is a good idea to park your car and travel by public transport. There are bus services in all towns and in Stockholm you can travel on the underground (Tunnelbana) which is one of the longest in the world with over 100km of track and is often beautifully decorated. In Göteborg there are still trams.

There is generally a flat-rate fare which entitles you to travel as far as you like. In Stockholm, Göteborg and Malmö you can buy special tourist tickets which enable you to travel as often as you like during the validity of the ticket. There is a special roundabout ticket in Stockholm – the so-called 'Stockholmskortet' which provides unlimited travel on all types of transport. It also provides free entry to over fifty sights in the city plus a number of bus and boat excursions. This ticket can be obtained at all tourist offices and bus depots and is valid for either 1 or 4 days.

There are bus tours of the city from the Opera House on Gustav Adolf's torg in Stockholm and boat tours from Nybroplan. There is also a ferry from here to Djurgården plus a number of boat excursions to the surrounding area.

Motoring in Sweden

There's nothing complicated about taking your car to Sweden. However, it is necessary to remember to take the following items:

1. A valid driving licence.
   Provisional driving licences are
   not valid.
2. Car logbook.
3. Certificate of vehicle insurance.
   A Green Card is not required but
   you are recommended to
   contact your insurance
   company for full policy
   protection.
4. A national identity plate.
5. Written authority to use the
   vehicle if you are not the owner.

Speed Limits
Speed limits on all roads are
indicated by road signs. Limits
outside built-up areas are 110, 90
or 70km/h. In built-up areas, the
limit is 50km/h. Watch out for signs
around school areas where the limit
is 30km/h. The speed limit for a car
towing a caravan outside built-up
areas is 70km/h if the caravan has
brakes, otherwise a speed limit of
40km/h applies. The same limit
applies to trailers.

Rules of the Road
You drive on the right in Sweden
and you must always give way to
traffic approaching from the right
unless road signs indicate
otherwise. You must always give
way to traffic already on a
roundabout.

Seat Belts
The driver and front seat
passenger must use seat belts and
back seat passengers are
recommended to use belts as well.
Children should be strapped in their
seats.

Lights
Dipped headlights are obligatory

when driving by day and by night.
Remember to have the beam of
your headlights adjusted to suit
right-hand driving if you are used to
driving on the left.

Road Conditions
Roads in the south of Sweden are
generally good but in the north
some roads are gravelled.
Motorists planning a trip to
Northern Sweden are
recommended to fit mud flaps to
the wheels and stoneguards on the
front of caravans. Winter driving
does not normally pose any serious
problems despite the weather
which can be expected. Roads are
cleared of snow quickly but it is
always necessary to look out for
black ice. Radial tyres or tyres with
an extra deep tread are advised.
Snow chains are not allowed on
main roads. Remember to put anti-
freeze in your windscreen water.

Fuel
Fuel is sold by the litre (1 gallon =
approx. 4.5 litres) and prices in
Sweden are still among the most
reasonable in Europe. There are
plenty of road-side filling stations
except in the north where it is
always advisable to carry a spare
can of fuel. Most filling stations are
self-service as indicated by the
sign 'Tanka Själv'. If you are driving
in country areas, remember that
filling stations generally close at
about 6pm. Many filling stations
have automatic pumps that accept
10 or 100skr notes where you can
fill up at any time of the day or night
and they are indicated by the sign.
'Sedel Automat' and fuel from these
pumps is slightly cheaper than
elsewhere. Lead-free fuel is

now available in most Swedish towns.

Parking
Parking regulations generally follow international practice. Vehicles must be parked on the right-hand side of the road but if you park in a street overnight look out for the sign indicating which night of the week the street is cleaned when you are not allowed to park. A circular sign with a red cross on a blue background surrounded by a red border indicates that parking is prohibited but if a yellow plate with a red border is added below the sign, it prohibits parking only during the time indicated. Parking meters are in use in large towns usually from 8am-6pm. The permitted parking time varies but is usually 2 hours. Fees vary from about 5 and 10skr per hour. Vehicles parked on inadequately lit roads must have their parking lights illuminated.
In Stockholm
Cars are the least convenient mode of transport in Stockholm. Car parks are inadequate and vehicles are banned from many of the streets. On the other hand, there are no great distances in the centre and all the most important sights can be reached on foot. Street parking overnight is on one side of the road only, which alternates so that streets can be cleaned. Information on this is given on signs at the street corners and on buildings and parking meters. Regulations must be strictly observed and offending vehicles are removed. If this happens, they can be repossessed at a centre in the north-western suburb of

Ropsen near the underground station of that name:
☎ (08) 542120 .

Breakdowns and Accidents
Contact either the police or the 'Larmjänst' organisation which is run by the Swedish insurance companies and has branches all over the country. It operates a 24-hour service and telephone numbers are listed in telephone directories. You can usually find the 'Larmjänst' number from petrol stations, police stations or taxi drivers. The emergency telephone number 90000 should only be used in the case of accidents, injury etc. Garages with repair facilities are usually open between 7am and 5pm but are often closed on Saturdays. A 24-hour emergency service is provided in most towns. It is not mandatory to call the police in the case of an accident but the drivers must give their names and addresses to the other parties involved.

Drinking and Driving
Sweden's laws on drink driving are strictly enforced and heavy fines are imposed. You can be prosecuted even if you have only a low level of alcohol in the blood (50mg/100ml – the equivalent of only two cans of beer).

Road Signs
Caution – Se upp, Giv akt
Customs – Tull
No entry – Infart förbjuden
One-way street – Enkelriktad
Road works – Vägarbete, Gatuarbete
Slow – Sakta
Stop – Stopp, Halt

Accommodation

Hotels and Motels
There is a good selection in all price categories in every Swedish town or city. Most are privately owned but some are operated by groups like Sara, Scandic, Inter S and Reso. Sweden Hotels is a group of 140 independently owned hotels with a central reservations office. In many areas special low rates may be obtained in July and August when most Swedish business executives are on holiday, and there are big reductions on weekend stays throughout the year. Motels are popular with families and are easy to reach. Some have swimming pools, gymnasiums, sauna, restaurants and self-service cafés. Most have family rooms with four beds.

For more detailed information about Discount Schemes, hotel facilities etc, travellers are advised to obtain a copy of 'Hotels in Sweden' from the Swedish National Tourist Office.

Self-Catering
Many Swedes own their own chalets or log cabins in the countryside and many chalets are available for rental. Standards of hygiene are high. Purpose-built chalets generally consist of a living room, two or three bedrooms, well-equipped kitchen and toilet, generally accommodate up to six people and cooking utensils, blankets, cutlery and pillows are provided. Visitors supply their own sheets and towels.

Log cabins offer simpler accommodation and they are usually sited in more remote spots, but again kitchen equipment, blankets and pillows are provided.

Sweden has about 250 chalet villages and all have grocery or general shops, some have restaurants, swimming pool, saunas, launderette, play-ground, mini-golf, and various other facilities including riding, fishing, dancing and barbecues.

Information on individual chalet holidays can be obtained from the Swedish National Tourist Office.

Budget Accommodation
Look for the 'Rum' sign or 'Room' – you get a room without breakfast. Local tourist offices have details of 'Rum' accommodation and prices are inexpensive. Special budget-priced bed and breakfast rates are available at 250 hotels, guesthouses and inns all over Sweden under a scheme designed for people on touring holidays. A number of farms throughout Sweden offer accommodation on a bed and breakfast basis with self-catering facilities for cooking other meals, some offering full board.

A list of farm accommodation is available from Landresor, Vasagatan 12, 01533 Stockholm, ☎ (08) 7875590. Or, contact the Swedish National Tourist Office.

Camping
There are more than 700 sites, all officially approved and classified by the Swedish Tourist Board. Many offer facilities like boat or bicycle hire, mini-golf or tennis, riding and saunas. Most authorised sites are open 1 June to 1 September. About 200 sites remain open in winter and about 180 offer

services for the disabled.

Camping holidays are inexpensive. Cyclists and walkers are often offered discounts. A camping carnet is needed at most sites (costing about 15skr); it is issued at the first site you visit and is valid for the whole season. The carnet is not required by holders of the 'Camping International' card.

Sites are awarded a one to three-star rating:

★ = daily inspection, barrier at entrance, dustbins, drinking water, toilets, washing facilities and hot water for dishwashing, laundry etc.
★★ = the above and supervision throughout the day, illuminated and fenced in area, drains for caravans, electricity for shaving, kiosk, foodstuffs, telephone and electric sockets for caravans.
★★★ = as above plus 24-hour supervision, postal service, car wash, café, cooking facilities, play and recreational areas and assembly room. An abbreviated list of campsites is available from the Swedish National Tourist Board.

Youth Hostels

The 280 youth hostels known as 'Vandrarhem' range from mansion houses, farms and medieval castles to renovated sailing ships. There are no restrictions — everyone welcome. Most have two or four beds or family rooms, self-catering facilities, and meals and light refreshments are provided in some. They are run by the STF (Swedish Touring Club) but if you are a member of the English, American or Scottish Youth Hostel Associations you qualify for a cheaper rate, so bring your

membership card with you. All hostels are open during the summer. A comprehensive list of youth hostels is available from the STF, Box 25, S-10120 Stockholm, or contact the Swedish National Tourist Office.

Tips for Travellers

Banking Hours

From 9.30am to 3pm, Monday to Friday usually. Closed Saturdays. In many large cities, banks close at 6pm. The Bank at Arlanda Airport in Stockholm is open from 7am to 10pm.

Shopping Hours

From 9am to 6pm, Monday to Friday and from 1pm until 4pm Saturdays. In country areas, shops and petrol stations close by 5-6pm. (For post office hours, see page 189.)

Passports

See page 188. A valid passport entitles you to a stay of up to 3 months. If you are planning to seek work in Sweden you should obtain a work permit from the Swedish Embassy.

Customs

In addition to the limits stated on page 188, all visitors over the age of 12 may import foods up to a limit of 15kg subject to certain limitations – no fresh, smoked or frozen meat may be imported but tinned meat is permitted. Within the overall 15kg allowance, only 5kg may be edible fats of which butter is limited to 2.5kg. Up to 5kg of fresh fruit and vegetables is permitted. Presents up to a value of 600skr may be imported but the value of any food is included in that limit. Medicine may be taken only if intended for the traveller's own use. Narcotics used as medicine may be taken in if intended for personal use for a period of no more than 5 days and if the traveller can produce a medical certificate.

No vaccinations are needed to travel to Sweden.

Exchange

See page 190 for currency and exchange rate details. Travellers cheques may be exchanged at banks all over Sweden and a foreign exchange service is also provided by some Post Offices with the 'PK Exchange' sign.

Swedish Time

One hour in advance of Greenwich Mean Time, ie it conforms to Central European Time. Clocks are put forward by 1 hour in summer (from the end of March to the end of September).

Credit Cards

Most international cards are welcome including Barclay Card, Visa, Access,Master-card/Eurocard, Diner's Club and American Express.

Discount Cards

Stockholm, Göteborg and Malmö have introduced special discount cards enabling you to make significant savings on sightseeing and shopping — the 'Stockholms-kortet' the 'Göteborgskortet' and the 'Malmökortet'. Contact the tourist information offices in these cities for details.

Facilities for the Disabled

Details on holidays and facilities for the disabled can be obtained from the Swedish National Tourist Office.

Telephones

Emergency number from anywhere in Sweden is 90000 (free of charge).

Dialling Codes (see p. 189):
From GB to Sweden: 01046
From US to Sweden: 01146

From Sweden to GB: 00944
From Sweden to US: 0091

When calling from an automatic payphone in Sweden, insert 1skr then wait for dialling tone before dialling your number. When you hear a signal during the call insert another coin if you wish to continue.

Tourist Information Offices

There are tourist information offices or 'Turistbyrå' in more than 300 locations throughout Sweden which can be identified by the international 'i' sign. They will be pleased to advise you on places of interest, recommended excursions, facilities for the disabled, and where to hire a bike or canoe. There is usually a hotel booking service too. Not all of them, however, are open daily, or indeed, all year so it is advisable to telephone before visiting.

Listed below are some of the major regional and area offices covered by *Visitor's Guide to Sweden.*

Regional Offices

Ångermanland
Box 77
87101 Härnösand
☎ (0611) 13030

Blekinge
Box 506
37123 Karlskrona
☎ (0455) 10582

Bohuslän
Box 56
45115 Uddevalla
☎ (0522) 14055

Dalarna
Tullkammaregatan 1
79131 Falun
☎ (023) 18740

Dalsland
Box 181
66200 Åmal
☎ (0532) 14366

Gotland
Box 2081
62102 Visby
☎ (0498) 19010

Gästrikland-Hälsingland
Hattmakareg 2
80351 Gävle
☎ (026) 129540

Halland
Box 68
30102 Halmstad
☎ (035) 114174

Härjedalen - Jämtland
83182 Östersund
☎ (063) 144001

Lapland
(Contact Norrbotten and Västerbotten Tourist Offices)

Medelpad
Box 77
87101 Härnösand
☎ (0611) 13030

Närke
Box 1816
70118 Örebro
☎ (019) 140070

Norrbotten
95184 Luleå
☎ (0920) 94070

Öland
Box 86
39121 Kalmar
☎ (0480) 28270

Östergötland
Box 176
58102 Linköping
☎ (013) 107600

Skåne
Stora Söderg 8c
22223 Lund
☎ (046) 124350

Småland
(Contact Tourist Offices at Växjö, Kalmar, Jönköping)

Södermanland
61188 Nyköping
☎ (0155) 45900

Uppland
Box 602
75125 Uppsala
☎ (018) 176000

Värmland
Box 323
65105 Karlstad
☎ (054) 102160

Västerbotten
Box 317
90107 Umeå
☎ (090) 139020

Västergötland
Box 213
54125 Skövde
☎ (0500) 18050

Västmanland
Hållgatan 2
72211 Västerås
☎ (021) 163000

Town and Area Offices

Åhus
Köpmannagatan 2
29600 Åhus
☎ (044) 11200

Alingsås
Konsthallen
44181 Alingsås
☎ (0322) 75200

Älvdalen
Dalgatan
79600 Älvdalen
☎ (0251) 10294

Alvesta
Centralgatan 6
34200 Alvesta
☎ (0472) 12260

Åmål
Åmål Marina
Södra Hamnplan 1
66200 Åmål
☎ (0532) 13860

Arboga
Box 45
Storatorget
73200 Arboga
☎ (0589) 14990

Arvika
Box 114
Stadsparken
67101 Arvika
☎ (0570) 13560

Avesta
Malmgatan 14
77400 Avesta
☎ (0226) 53420

Backe
Box 81
Stenhammarn
88050 Backe
☎ (0624) 10543

Bengtsfors
Torget
66600 Bengtsfors
☎ (0531) 11665

Boden
Stadshuset
96185 Boden
☎ (0921) 50160

Borgholm
Hamnen
Box 115
38700 Borgholm
☎ (0485) 12340

Borlänge
Borganäsvägen 25
78131 Borlänge
☎ (0243) 18125

Boxholm
Torget
59010 Boxholm
☎ (0142) 51080

Dalarö
Odinsvägen 3
13054 Dalarö
☎ (0750) 50800

Enköping
Idrottshuset
19880 Enköping
☎ (0171) 30569

Eskilstuna
Fristadstorget 5
63107 Eskilstuna
☎ (016) 102250

Falkenberg
Box 293
Holgersgatan 22B
31101 Falkenberg
☎ (0346) 17410

Falsterbo
Box 122
Ljungens Campingplats
23010 Skanör
☎ (040)473508

Falun
Stora Torget
79183 Falun
☎ (023) 83637

Filipstad
Box 303
Vikgatan, Folkets Hus
68201 Filipstad
☎ (0590) 11560

Gävle
Box 175
Stortorget
80103 Gävle
☎ (026) 101600

Göteborg
Kungsportsplatsen 2
41110 Göteborg
☎ (031) 100740

Gränna
Box 104
Torget
56300 Gränna
☎ (0390) 10315

Grums
Box 44
Sveagatan 77-85
66400 Grums
☎ (0555) 11694/13508

Halmstad
Box 47
Kajplan
30102 Halmstad
☎ (035) 109345

Hede
Box 157
Hede Camping
B2093 Hede
☎ (0684) 11080

Hedemora
Box 32
Callerholmsgatan 6
77600 Hedemora
☎ (0225) 10100/34000

Helsingborg
Rådhuset
25221 Helsingborg
☎ (042) 120310

Hudiksvall
Box 149
Möljen
82401 Hudiksvall
☎ (0650) 13920

Idre
Kommunalhuset
79091 Idre
☎ (0253) 20710

Jokkmokk
Box 36
Porjusvägen 4
96040 Jokkmokk
☎ (0971) 17227/12140

Jönköping
Västra Storgatan 9
55189 Jönköping
☎ (036) 105050

Kalmar
Box 23
Larmgatan 6
39120 Kalmar
☎ (0480) 15350

Karslborg
Ñorra Kanalgatan 2
54600 Karlsborg
☎ (0505) 12120

Karlshamn
Drottninggatan 54
29200 Karlshamn
☎ (0454) 16595

Karlskoga
Centralplan 1
69183 Karlskoga
☎ (0586) 56348

Karlskrona
Box 10
Södra Smedjegatan 6
37121 Karlskrona
☎ (0455) 83490/83000

Karlstad
Tingvallagatan ID/S Kyrkog 10
65184 Karlstad
☎ (054) 19501

Katrineholm
Box 901
Stortorget
64129 Katrineholm
☎ (0150) 57241

Kiruna
Hjalmar Lundbomsväg 42
98185 Kiruna
☎ (0980) 18880

Klintehamn
Donnerska Huset
62020 Klintehamn
☎ (0498) 40308

Kolmården
Kolmården Djurpark
68100 Kolmården
☎ (011) 95006

Kopparberg
Box 52
Tinghuset, Gruvstugetorget
☎ (0580) 10439

Kristianstad
V. Boulevarden 15
29131 Kristianstad
☎ (044) 121988

Kristinehamn
Box 45
Västerlånggatan 22
68101 Kristinehamn
☎ (0550) 10573

Kronoberg
Box 36
S-35103 Växjö
☎ (0470) 47575

Kungälv
Fästningsholmen
44231 Kungälv
☎ (0303) 12035

Kungsbacka
Storgatan 41
43400 Kungsbacka
☎ (0300) 34619

Laholm
Stadshuset
31201 Laholm
☎ (0430) 15450

Landskrona
Rådhusgatan 3
26131 Landskrona
☎ (0418) 16980

Leksand
Box 52
Norsgatan
79301 Leksand
☎ (0247) 80300

Lidköping
Gamla Rådhuset
53131 Lidköping
☎ (0510) 83500

Linköping
Ågatan 39
58101 Linköping
☎ (013) 206835/206050

Ljungby
Gamla Torg
34100 Ljungby
☎ (0372) 13404

Luleå
Rådstugatan 9
95135 Luleå
☎ (0920) 93746/93829

Lund
Box 1105
Kattesund 6
22104 Lund
☎ (046) 124590/155963

Lycksele
Storgatan 29
92100 Lycksele
☎ (0950) 10495

Malmö
Hamngatan 1
21122 Malmö
☎ (040) 341270

Malung
Grönlandsvägen 24
78200 Malung
☎ (0280) 11811

Mariefred
Rådhuset
15030 Mariefred
☎ (0159) 10207

Mariestad
Hamnplanen
54200 Mariestad
☎ (0501) 10001

Markaryd
Drottninggatan 2
28500 Markaryd
☎ (0433) 11166

Mellerud
Gamla Tingshuset, by road 45
46400 Mellerud
☎ (0530) 11670

Mjölby
Stora Torget
59500 Mjölby
☎ (0142) 17573

Mönsterås
Torget 20
38300 Mönsterås
☎ (0499) 13001

Mora
Ångbåtskajen
79200 Mora
☎ (0250) 26550

Motala
Folkets Hus
Sjög 5
59130 Motala
☎ (0141) 17573

Nordmaling
Rödviken
91400 Nordmaling
☎ (0930) 10750

Norrköping
Drottninggatan 18
60181 Norrköping
☎ (011) 151500

Norrtälje
Box 200
Lilla Torget
76100 Norrtälje
☎ (0176) 13700/71175

Norsjö
Storgatan 67
93500 Norsjö
☎ (0918) 10331

Nyköping
Stora Torget
61183 Nyköping
☎ (0155) 81274

Nynäshamn
14981 Nynäshamn
☎ (0752) 12131

Örebro
Drottninggatan 9
70210 Örebro
☎ (019) 130760

Örkelljunga
Stockholmsvägen 7/stationen
28600 Örkelljunga
☎ (0435) 50477

Oskarshamn
Box 6
Ö Torgg 13, Stora Torget
57201 Oskarshamn
☎ (0491) 88188

Oxelösund
Järntorget
61301 Oxelösund
☎ (0155) 33743

Piteå
Industrigatan 44
94185 Piteå
☎ (0911) 19755

Rättvik
Box 90
Torget
79500 Rättvik
☎ (0248) 10910/10645

Ronneby
Box 114
Snäckebacksplan
37200 Ronneby
☎ (0457) 17650

Säffle
Billerudsg. 5-7
66100 Säffle
☎ (0533) 10600

Sala
Box 76
Gillegatan
73300 Sala
☎ (0224) 13600

Sandviken
Baldersplan 1
81180 Sandviken
☎ (026) 241380

Sigtuna
Box 78
Drakegården
19300 Sigtuna
☎ (0760) 51432

Simrishamn
Tullhusgatan 2
27200 Simrishamn
☎ (0414) 10666

Skara
Skolgatan 1
53200 Skara
☎ (0511) 14470/14426

Skellefteå
Informationscentralen, Storg 46
93131 Skellefteå
☎ (0910) 58880

Skövde
Box 83 Sandtorget
54122 Skövde
☎ (0500) 80517

Söderhamn
Oxtorgsgatan 14
82600 Söderhamn
☎ (0270) 11862

Söderköping
Box 100
Rådhuset
61400 Söderköping
☎ (0121) 12940/18160

Södertälje
Centralstationen
Järnagatan 11
15189 Södertälje
☎ (0755) 22300/18899

Sölvesborg
Box 30
Skånevågen 30
29401 Sölvesborg
☎ (0456) 10088

Sorsele
Box 101
Stationsgatan
92070 Sorsele
☎ (0952) 10900

Stockholm
Box 7542
Sverigehuset Kungsträdgården
10393 Stockholm
☎ (08) 7892000

Storuman
Box 84
Höjdvägen
92300 Storuman
☎ (0951) 10500

Strängnäs
Västerviken
15200 Strängnäs
☎ (0152) 13400

Strömstad
Box 76
Norra Hamnen
45201 Strömstad
☎ (0526) 13030

Sundsvall
Torget
85230 Sundsvall
☎ (060) 114235/117893

Sunne
Box 139
Mejerig 2, Sunne Turistcentrum
68600 Sunne
☎ (0565) 10681/11411

Tanumshede
Box 113
Affärsvägen 16
45700 Tanumshede
☎ (0525) 29060

Tärnaby
V. Strandvägen 11
92064 Tärnaby
☎ (0954) 10450

Töreboda
Gästhamnen
54500 Töreboda
☎ (0506) 10130

Torsby
Box 1
Gamla Torget
68500 Torsby
☎ (0560) 10550/10500

Trelleborg
Garvaregården
23100 Trelleborg
☎ (0410) 42120

Trollhättan
Malgöbron
46181 Trollhättan
☎ (0520) 14025

Trosa
Torget
15013 Trosa
☎ (0156) 16170

Uddevalla
Södra Hamnen 2
45181 Uddevalla
☎ (0522) 11787

Umeå
Renmarkstorget
90247 Umeå
☎ (090) 161616

Uppsala
Box 216
Smedsgränd 7
75104 Uppsala
☎ (018) 117500/161825

Vadstena
Box 16
Rådhustorget
59200 Vadstena
☎ (0143) 10250

Vaggeryd
Jönköpingsvägen 77
56700 Vaggeryd
☎ (0393) 12323

Valdemarsvik
Centralplan
61500 Valdermarsvik
☎ (0381) 60330/60335

Vänersborg
Ursand
☎ (0521) 18666

Vännäs
Förargatan 1
91100 Vännäs
☎ (0935) 20782

Varberg
Box 150
Brunnsparken
43202 Varberg
☎ (0340) 88770

Värnarmo
Apladalen
33100 Värnarmo
☎ (0370) 12346

Västerås
Stora torget
72215 Västerås
☎ (021) 161830

Västervik
Strömsholmen
59300 Västervik
☎ (0490) 13695/16920

Växjö
Box 1222
Kronobergsgatan 8
35112 Växjö
☎ (0470) 41410/41000

Vaxholm
Box 17
Söderhamnsplan
18500 Vaxholm
☎ (0764) 31480/31500

Vilhelmina
Storgatan 17
91200 Vilhelmina
☎ (0940) 11100/11101

Visingsö
Hamnen
56000 Visingsö
☎ (0390) 40193

Ydre
57060 Österbymo
☎ (0381) 60330

Useful Addresses and Telephone Numbers

Travel Information

Association of Swedish Travel
  Agents
Engelbrektsplan 2
S-11434 Stockholm
☎ (08) 233130

British Airways
Norrmalstorg 7
Stockholm
☎ (08) 233900

DFDS Seaways (GB)
Tyne Commission Quay
North Shields, NE29 6EE
☎ (91) 257 5655

DFDS Seaways (GB)
Scandinavia House
Parkeston Quay
Harwich
Essex, CO12 4QG
☎ (0255) 554681

DFDS Seaways (GB)
Scandinavia House
Parkeston Quay
Harwich
Essex, CO12 4QG
☎ (0255) 554681

DFDS Seaways
Hotellplatsen 2
41106 Göteborg
☎ (031) 172050

DFDS Seaways
Birger Jarlsgatan 6
11434 Stockholm
☎ (08) 241880

Fred Olsen Travel (GB)
11 Conduit Street
London W1R 0LS
☎ (01) 409 3275

Lion Ferry AB
Box 94
s-432 02 Varberg
☎ (0340) 19010

Linjeflyg (domestic flights)
Box 20150
s-16120 Bromma
☎ (08) 240020/225940

Norwegian State Railways (GB)
 (agents for Swedish State
 Railways)
21/24 Cockspur Street
London SW1
☎ (01) 930 6666

Olau Line (GB)
Olau Line Terminal
Sheerness
Kent ME12 1SN
☎ (0795) 666666

Pan Am Airlines
Jakobstorg 1
Stockholm
☎ (08) 231920

SAS Scandinavian Airlines (GB)
52/53 Conduit Street
London WIR 0AY
☎ (01) 734 4020

SAS Scandinavian Airlines
Flygcity
Sveavägen 22
Stockholm
☎ (08) 7801000

Scandinavian Express (Tours)
 (USA)
Scandinavian Marketing Services
535 Broad Hollow Road
Suite B34
Melville NY 11747
☎ (516) 752 9411

Stena Line AB
Box 31300
40032 Göteborg
☎ (031) 420940

Swedish State Railways (ST)
Centralhuset
s-10550 Stockholm
☎ (08) 762 2000

Townsend Thoreson (GB)
127 Regent Street
London W1
☎ (01) 4375641

Viking Line (GB)
c/o Scantours
8 Spring Gardens
London SW1
☎ (01) 8392927

Advice for Travellers

American Youth Hostels, Inc.
1332 "I" Street N.W.
Washington D.C. 20005
☎ (202) 7836161

British Embassy
Skarpögatan 6-8
Stockholm
☎ (08) 670140

Caravan Club (GB)
East Grinstead House
East Grinstead
West Sussex RH19 IUA
☎ (0342) 26944

International Youth Centre
Valhallavägen 142
s-11524 Stockholm
☎ (08) 634389

Scandinavian National Tourist
Offices (Denmark-Sweden)
 (USA)
8929 Wilshire Blvd
Beverley Hills
California 90211
☎ (213) 854 1549

Scandinavian National Tourist
Offices (Denmark-Sweden)
 (USA)
150 North Michigan Avenue
Suite 2110
Chicago
Illinois 6061
☎ (312) 726 1120

SFS-Resor
 (Swedish National Student Travel
 Bureau)
Drottninggatan 89
Box 45072
10430 Stockholm
☎ (08) 340180

STF Swedish Touring Association
Vasagatan 48
Box 25
s-10120 Stockholm
☎ (08) 227200

Swedish Cycling Association
Box 6006
16306 Spänga
☎ (08) 7516204

Swedish Embassy (GB)
11 Montagu Place
London W1
☎ (01) 724 2101

Swedish Embassy (US)
Watergate 600
Suite 1200
600 New Hampshire Avenue North
 West
Washington D.C. 20037
☎ (202) 944 5600

Swedish Institute
Box 7434
s-103 91 Stockholm
☎ (08) 7892000

Swedish National Tourist Office
3 Cork Street
London W1X 1HA
☎ (01) 437 5816

Swedish Radio Authority
 (permission for CB's)
Televerkets Radiodivision
Tillståndskontoret
s-12386 Stockholm

Swedish Tourist Board
Hamngatan 27
Stockholm
☎ (08) 221840

Swedish Tourist Board
655 Third Avenue
New York NY10017
☎ (212) 949 2333

Tourist Information Centre
Sweden House
Kungsträdsgården
Stockholm
☎ (08) 7892000

US Embassy
Strandvägen 101
Stockholm
☎ (08) 630520

Accommodation

Hotellcentralen
 (Service for hotels and rooming
 houses)
Central Railway Station
Stockholm
☎ (08) 240880

Landresor (Farm House Holidays)
Vasagatan 12
s-10533 Stockholm
☎ (08) 7875100

SCR Swedish Campsite Owners
 Association
Box 255
s-45117 Uddevalla
☎ (0522) 39345

Svenska Turistföreningen STF
 (YHA)
Box 25
s-10120 Stockholm
☎ (08) 010468/227200

YHA (England & Wales)
14 Southampton Street
London WC2E 7HE
☎ (01) 8368541

Car Hire

Avis Rent-a-Car
Albygatan 109B
s-17154 Solna
☎ (08) 290909

Esso Biluthyrning
Box 5833
s-10248 Stockholm
☎ (08) 639282

Hertz-Volvohandelns Biluthyrning
Mäster Samuelsgatan 67
s-11121 Stockholm
☎ (08) 240720

Inter Rent Biluthyrning
Box 7545
s-10393 Stockholm
☎ (08) 240280

Bicycle Rentals

Cykelspecialisten: Hoj In
Karlbergsvägen 55
Stockholm
☎ (08) 345758

**Mobile Homes and Caravan
 Hire**

Bil AB Olle Björklund
Kennil Marketing
Östra Ringgatan 1
s-44131 Alingsås
☎ (0322) 15950

BP Hjällbo
Box 2030
s-42402 Angered
☎ (031) 468790

Husvagnsuthyrning AB
Kranvägen 6
s-19454 Upplands Väsby
☎ (0760) 89100

Josefsons Husvagn
Box 39
s-43801 Landvetter
☎ (031) 710703

Sakiva
Kopparbergsgatan 17/19
s-21444 Malmö
☎ (040) 83643

Sweden Mobile Camper
Kyrkovägen 10
s-43333 Partille
☎ (031) 443035

Wiksenius Husvagnar AB
Ridspögatan 4
s-21377 Malmö
☎ (040) 222525

Åby Fritid
Box 76
s-61600 Åby
☎ (011) 63025

Motoring Organisations

Kungliga Automobilklubben
 (Royal Automobile Club)
Södra Blasieholmshamn–6
Box 5855
s-10248 Stockholm 16
☎ (08) 238800
(offices in Göteborg and Malmö)

Motormännens Riksförbund (M)
 (National Motorists' Association)
Sturegatan 32
s-10240 Stockholm 5
☎ (08) 670580
(Offices in Eskilstuna, Göteborg,
Helsingborg, Jönköping, Luleå,
Malmö, Norrköping, Örebro,
Östersund, Skövde, Söderhamn,
Sundsvall, Uppsala, Västerås

Help in Stockholm
Arlanda Airport
 ☎ (08) 7803030/7805000
Breakdown ☎ (08) 241000
Boat excursions
 ☎ (08) 140830
Campsites Ängby Camping,
 Bromma ☎ (08) 370420
 Bredäng Camping, Skärholmen
 ☎ (08) 977071
 Rösjöns Camping, Sollentuna
 ☎ (08) 353475

Emergency (fire, accident,
 ambulance) ☎ 90000 (free of
 charge)
Local transport (buses, trains,
 boats) ☎ (08) 236000
Long-distance trains
 ☎ (08) 7622000
Lost property Central Station
 ☎ (08) 7622000
 Police Station, Tjärhovsgatan 21
 ☎ (08) 410432
 Stockholm Transit Company (SL)
 Rådmansgatan, Tunnelbanstation
 ☎ (08) 7360780
Pharmacist C.W. Scheele,
 Klarabergsgatan 64
 ☎ (08) 248280
Police Agnegatan 33-37
 ☎ (08) 693000
Post Office Vasagatan 28-34
 ☎ (08) 7812000
Taxi ☎ (08) 150000
Tourist Information
 ☎ (08) 7892000
Youth hostels Chapman,
 Skeppsholmen ☎ (08) 202506
 Hantverkshuset, Skeppsholmen
 ☎ (08) 202506
 Zinken, Pipmakargränd 2
 ☎ (08) 685786

INDEX

Index to Places

Swedish dictionaries place **å**, **ä** and **ö** (in that order) at the end of the alphabet after **z**. But for the purposes of this index they have been treated as **aa**, **ae** and **oe**. The Norwegian characters **æ** and **ø** have similarly been treated as **ae** and **oe**.

Index to Subjects